Stories from Home

JERRY CLOWER
STORIES
· · · · · · from · · · · · ·
HOME

University Press of Mississippi
Jackson

www.upress.state.ms.us

The University Press of Mississippi is a member
of the Association of American University Presses.

2011 paperback edition © by Jerry Clower
All rights reserved
Manufactured in the United States of America

Paperback ISBN 978-1-61703-070-3
Ebook ISBN 978-1-61703-071-0

∞

Designed by John Langston

Library of Congress Cataloging-in-Publication Data

Clower, Jerry, 1926–
Stories from home / Jerry Clower.
p. cm.
ISBN 0-87805-547-9
1. Clower, Jerry, 1926– . 2. Comedians—United States—
Biography. I. Title.
PN2287.C547A3   1992
813'.54—dc20   91-38118
                                                              CIP

British Library Cataloging-in-Publication Data available

To the memory of my mother
Jacqueline B. Moore
1908–1991
who taught me perseverance,
loyalty, and love

Contents

Contents

A Family Named Ledbetter

Me and Marcel

Contents

God's Gonna Take Care of Me

Mama's Deal and Other Family Matters

Contents

Contents

Proud to Be an American

Foreword

by Willie Morris

The comic art of Jerry Clower reveals, and is undergirded by, the richness of the spoken language of the American South in all its inwardness and nuance and sweep—the extravagant country talk, as lyrical as much of southern literature, and in the lineal ancestry of southern writing. "I don't tell funny stories," he is wont to say, "I tell stories funny." He does both. He is not just a big mirthful fellow in an outrageous red suit. "Clower is serious about his story-telling," the compendious *Encyclopedia of Southern Culture* affirms for us, "and the cultural heritage and Christian tradition from which he springs." All our distinguished American humorists have been serious people, their hearts as rueful as they are merry. "I'm funny because I'm sad," it was attributed to Mark Twain, "and I'm sad because I'm funny."

Jerry Clower is an artist of deep values, values which yet exist in our civilization: hard work, loyalty, honesty, community, family, friendship, generosity, love, and, withal, a vibrant aversion to the hypocritical, the bogus, and the unpitying, not to mention an instinctual distaste for cynical barbers, dilatory hitchhikers, and all souls of greed. He understands the world because he has assiduously lived it. He knows what he is talking about.

He knows, too, America, its loneliness and fears, its complexity and promise. He is not a stranger to the American road. His humor is rooted in a region, but is not regional. "There's no more North, South, East, and West as we once knew it," he has said. "If they laugh at it in Birmingham, they'll laugh at it in Boston. I go everywhere, and they laugh everywhere." His ineradicable cast of humanity is a universal cosmos: Marcel, Newgene, Aunt Pet and Uncle Versie Ledbetter, Clovis Ledbetter, and Clovis' wife Azlee, the world's ugliest woman ("If Moses had seen Azlee, there'd have been another commandment").

From Jerry Clower's prolific tales many of us are familiar with his sources: a seventeen-year-old mother, a father who deserted them, the bone-crushing Depression poverty in the unrelenting earth of southern Mississippi. His county was so poor, he said, that most people could not even afford to sin. He ate so much slick, shiny boiled okra when he was a boy he could never keep his socks up. He was baptized at thirteen in the Amite River near the old East Fork Baptist Church. His mother had to labor hard to keep her boys from foster homes. "I've seen her pick two rows of cotton, and working and knocking off about eleven thirty to go to the house and try to scrape up something to eat—some hoecake or something out of an old meal barrel."

He was raised also by dogs, for whom he nurtured an abidingly uncanny and affectionate appreciation. Their names were Old Brummy, Little Red, Old Jennie, Old Tory, Old Big Red, Mike, and Little Red, the latter of whom owed his life after an injury to the succor of a kindly druggist in McComb, Mississippi. "Why, I wouldn't be here today if it weren't for them pack of dogs," he would remember, "because they put meat on the table. I'm not so sure that none of us have ever been loved by an earthly creature until we have been loved by a dog." Children likewise would have a special place in his work, and he subscribed in his own heart to the great Tom T. Hall's affecting testimonial: "Little children are still too young to hate," and "Ain't but three things in this world that's worth a solitary dime: old dogs and children and watermelon wine."

After his tenure in the Navy in World War II Jerry studied agriculture at Mississippi State. As with one of his heroes, Bear Bryant, the first football game he had ever seen he played in. Later he was a 233-pound tackle for State. "Nowadays," he said, "they got running backs bigger than I was back then." He was an assistant county agent in Oxford, Mississippi, and then a fertilizer salesman for the Mississippi Chemical Corporation in Yazoo City, where he at first lectured potential customers on how his firm made "homogenized, homogenous, water soluble, pelletized fertilizers." When this failed to work, the fledgling entrepreneur began telling them country stories. One of his clients recorded him and took the tape to Hollywood. An agent telephoned him. "The next time you're in the vicinity of the West Coast," the agent said, "please drop by." Jerry replied: "I ain't never gonna be in that vicinity. Fellow, you don't leave Yazoo City, Mississippi, and just drop by Los Angeles." With the encouragement of the saintly and heroic Owen Cooper, his employer at Mississippi Chemical, he tried his hand at story-telling for a living.

Nor is it by any means astonishing that Jerry Clower honors the literary tradition of his native state. Brother Will Campbell, his cousin-in-law, grew up a mile down the road in East Fork and taught Jerry how to tie a Windsor knot in a tie. Will "was thirty years ahead of his time on how to treat black people," Jerry remembered, "but he can describe in detail how to make molasses, clean chitterlings, or sharpen a hoe." Jerry had conversations with William Faulkner when he was county agent in Oxford, which also comes as no surprise to me: the two men shared an interest in trees and grass and growing things, as well as in dogs, rabbits, coons, mules, and human beings. The story of their mutual friend John Cullen of Oxford writing the King of Sweden suggesting he feed Bill Faulkner collards and opossum during his sojourn to accept the Nobel Prize, and the King of Sweden's reply, has its place in these pages.

Among Jerry's most valuable contributions as a public figure, and as an individual, has been his eloquent and unstinting position on behalf of racial equality and understanding in Mississippi and elsewhere, a belief he would consider integral to his own practicing religion. "It's still a mystery to me," he would say, "how godly people can tithe their income, give to the poor, read the Bible, pray, love folks, and let God run every fiber of their being except how they treat black people." When the citizens of Yazoo City not long ago chose to name a good portion of Highway 49 that runs along the town Jerry Clower Boulevard, there was a symbolic resonance in the appellation, immensely gratifying to the namesake, because Highway 49 links up not many miles south, along a lengthy stretch of that artery in Jackson, to Medgar Evers Boulevard: a white and a black arm, in the A.D. 1990s in his beloved Mississippi, reaching out to each other.

Jerry's hard-earned artistry is revered and enjoyed by a broad spectrum of his fellows. His record albums, for instance, sell more than those of all other American entertainers combined in the truck stops of the nation. The truckers, a restless and lonely and uncommon American breed, savor his thoughts and tales; he makes them want to be better. In his work and in his example he has been a civilizing influence in the South and the nation on those things that matter deeply. Even at his most uproarious his humor has been characterized by a commitment to an older and more elusive America whose expressed ideals of democratic justice and humility touched somehow the unsophisticated young men and women in its provinces and shaped them into maturity: a faith that poverty could be overcome and that one would be the stronger for having experienced it; an uncompromising regard for the underdog and the dispossessed; for the wayward tramp; for the lost brother; an allegiance to free expression and a hope that in the discord of hardy voices some truth might prevail; an almost mystical country boy's faith that this nation is a last great hope of the world—and running through all these, of course, the wonderful restorative gift of his laughter. I hope Mississippi, the South, and America know whom they have in my friend Jerry Clower. I believe they do.

Jackson, Mississippi
December 1991

ALL I AM

A Conversation with Jerry Clower

My granddaddy would be proud that I have a happy home and that I live where my roots are, that I still get excited when a neighbor brings me a mess of peas, and that I still love to go down and look at the baptizing hole where it all started.

In 1988 Jerry Clower and his wife Homerline moved from Yazoo City, Mississippi, back to East Fork community in Amite County, Mississippi—the place of his birth and boyhood and the source of much of his personal strength and many of his stories. Their new home at One Amazing Grace Lane is a spacious, brick country house with a deep porch extending across the front, where a row of oversized rocking chairs beckons the visitor. Here, in the summer of 1991, Jerry Clower talked about the people and events that have inspired and moved him, both as a man and as an entertainer, about his career, and about his personal convictions.

Jerry, will you review how you got started in show business?

Well, it all started when I was nine years old. I grew up at Route 4, Liberty, Mississippi. I was in the third grade, and the teacher made an announcement. She said, "All of you boys who are interested in joining the 4-H Club, go in the study hall. Well, I didn't know what the 4-H Club was, but I'dv got out of her class for a few minutes if they'd said, "Go fight a bear." So, I went in the study hall and this tall red-headed fellow got up and said, "Boys, I am the 4-H Club agent."

He explained to us what the 4-H Club was. He said we could have a project, and I selected a project in soil conservation. I planted *Zereesha lespedeza*—set out loblolly pines and locust trees in my project of soil conservation. At age thirteen I won the district competition, and a trip to Gulfport, Mississippi. I was so impressed with the 4-H Club agent, I wanted to grow up to be like him.

I went off and fought a war, I got my discharge, and went back home. When I walked up in the yard, my mama said, "Baby, what you gonna do the rest of your life?"

I said, "I'm gonna be a 4-H Club agent."

She said, "Hon, you can't be a 4-H Club agent unless you get a degree in agriculture."

Well, that was my motivation to get an education. I worked my way through Mississippi State University playing football. The first big-time college football game I ever played in on the road was in Knoxville, Tennessee. I run out on that field and I got so excited, I thought my heart was going to bust. And when Doug Atkins drew back and popped me up 'side the head one time, I was hoping it would bust.

But I got a degree in agriculture from Mississippi State University. The first job I ever had I was assistant county agent at Oxford, Mississippi. I had fulfilled my life's ambition. I had that job two years, and I was offered a job selling fertilizer for Mississippi Chemical Corporation, with the understanding I could still do public relations for the 4-H Club.

I went into the fertilizer business, and I traveled on the road selling fertilizer and making talks. I would tell them how we made "homogenized, homogeneous, water soluble, pelletized fertilizers." But I never did get invited back!

So, I started telling some country stories. An old boy said, "Hey, I heard you talk to them farmers. Why don't you make a record?"

I said, "You crazy, I ain't studyin' no record."

He said, "Well, you gonna tell them bloomin' stories anyhow. The next time you talk to a group of farmers, do you care if I tape it?"

I said, "I don't care what you do."

Well, he taped it and went to Hollywood and played it for MCA Records, and, hey, they done called me on the phone.

"Mr. Clower?"

I said, "Yes?"

"You have some possibilities. We've heard your work. We don't have a humorist on our label. We'd like very much to negotiate with you. The next time you're in the vicinity of the West Coast, please drop by."

I said, "I ain't never gonna be in that vicinity. Fellow, you don't leave Yazoo City, Mississippi, and just drop by Los Angeles."

He said, "We'd like very much to sign you to a five-year contract. To tell you the truth, Mr. Clower, our number one artists at the present time are Elton John, Sonny and Cher, Roger Williams, Ricky Nelson, plus many, many others."

I said, "Name some of them many, many others."

He said, "Conway Twitty, Loretta Lynn, Jeannie Pruett, Bill Monroe, and Ernest Tubb."

Ernest Tubb! I said, "Man, every Saturday night when I was grow-ing up we used to go to whoever's house had the strongest battery on their radio, and we would tune in to the Grand Ole Opry and we'd listen to Mr. Tubb. We'd turn the radio up loud and then snatch the knobs off where nobody could move it off that station."

I signed a five-year contract with MCA Records in 1970. Thirty days later I had a gold record.

When did you start telling stories? When did you first realize that you could tell stories and people would laugh?

The first time I ever remember being requested to tell a story was when I was in the navy. I was standing in a chow line on the U.S.S. *Bennington CV20*—an aircraft carrier in the South Pacific—fight-ing a war. An old boy come up to me and said, "Hey, rebel, you remember this morning when we was in the chow line at breakfast and you told me what you and Marcel Ledbetter would be doing at the swimming hole if y'all was home today? Tell my buddy." I had to think to remember what I told him.

Then when I got out of the navy and went to work, I would tell country stories to improve my sales technique, and that's the way I actually backed into show business.

Was it difficult to switch careers?

The key to me being successful in show business, in my opinion, comes from one man, Mr. Owen Cooper. When I made that first record and it was a hit, Mr. Cooper, president of Mississippi Chemical Corporation and my boss, called me to his office and said, "Jerry, what's happening to you could be tremendous or it could blow over. Your company is willing to share you for a while until you see which way you want to go. Don't be nervous and uptight about it." If he had called me in and said, "Make up your mind whether you're going to sell fertilizer or get into show business," I probably would have stayed in fertilizer because I knew I could make a living for my family that way.

But after about six months, I got to be a special guest on the Grand Ole Opry, and Mr. Cooper said, "We'll just make you director of sales promotion and pay you just enough to keep up your Blue Cross. Who do you suggest to take your place?"

Here was a man who practiced what he preached. And I've been associated with Mississippi Chemical ever since.

Why do you like being a country entertainer?

What I like the most about being a country entertainer is that I have an opportunity to perform before families. I'm a family entertainer. I like to see mamas and daddies and boys and girls come together and laugh together. I feel like for forty-five minutes or an hour they can forget the interest rates, and they can forget about the car payment. The audience can giggle and grin and laugh with old Jerry.

When I went to the Coastal Carolina Fair at Charleston, I literally shed tears when I landed because of the devastation of Hurricane Hugo—beautiful timber just ripped asunder. But I go out there to perform that evening at seven and nine, and they've got standing room only—in the rain, on a cold night. I know that they've been working with them chain saws and they've been worried with them insurance folks, but they see where ole Jerry is coming to town and they say, "I owe this to myself. I'm just going to see Jerry and to laugh." That's what is right about this business. I don't have any complaints about this business because I don't know enough about it to criticize it, to tell you the truth.

The Grand Ole Opry—I take being a member of that real seriously. I love it! They claim if you are in country music, that's the ultimate: you can't go no higher than that. And I've been a member of the world-famous Grand Ole Opry since 1973. You know this is such a great country!

They told me, "Jerry, MCA's got you on the 'David Frost Show' in New York City."

So, I go up there and David Frost said, "You're like a breath of fresh air to come in on the scene. I never interview anybody in show business that we don't talk about how much alimony they pay. You mean you married your childhood sweetheart and you are still together? Can you come back tomorrow?"

I stayed with MCA records and got to where I liked it. At first they said, "Jerry, unless you put a little risque or vulgar stuff on your records, you ain't never going to be known nationally." But I defied them: I have never used risque material.

When I signed with MCA and went to Nashville, and they gave me all that money, I called my wife, Homerline, and said, "Honey, I don't know what's happening to me, but if it comes between me and you, I'll lay it down." And today—twenty-two years later—we couldn't be happier. An old preacher one time said, "You ought to do right cause it's right to do right." That's just what I want to say.

Well, now I got twenty-one albums on MCA, and I've just cut two home videos. I've been on MCA longer than any other artist.

You have spoken often about growing up poor. How did poverty shape your beliefs and career?

Well, I was born in the quarters of a sawmill, and my father drove a truck and hauled lumber and logs—this was just before the Great

Depression. My father left my mother and my brother and me. We didn't have any way to make a living, so we moved in with my grandfather. My mama was a teenager with two children and no education. We tried to make a crop. I remember no electricity, no running water, no telephones, and dirt roads; but we didn't feel sorry for ourselves because nobody had telephones. I didn't really find out I was that poor until I joined the navy and saw three meals a day and calisthenics and all this. But I would have eat a little more at times had I had it.

My poor upbringing has been some of my motivation when I start to thinking that my work is good enough when maybe I don't want to re-do part of an album. I remember Charlie Pride telling me one time that when he gets tired and don't think he is up to performing, or he wants to cut his show short, he remembers picking cotton at Marks, Mississippi. And he would never want to go back.

I don't ever want to ever, never see my family or anybody be in the situation I grew up in. I think that's why I put on tournaments and do benefits to try to help people.

What were the worst things about being poor?

They'd make an announcement in the school that next Monday afternoon Buffalo Joe is coming and he's got a dog that'll jump through a hoop and he takes a whip and does things with that whip. And if you want to see him, you bring a nickel. And sitting down there during the program in the third grade by ourselves usually would be just me and my brother, because we didn't have a nickel.

And I hated seeing my mother work so hard, seeing her get out in the field and try to scrape up something to eat and get us school clothes and books—there weren't free books then.

I used to resent going down the highway by Fernwood Country Club out from McComb and seeing them folks playing golf. I hated them—which was wrong. I grew in grace and quit hating them. But I didn't think anybody ought to have had time to go up there and take a dern golf club and knock a little ball around and then sit in the shade and drink iced tea.

What if you hadn't been poor? Could you have achieved what you have?

No. Because I would have probably been arrogant and I wouldn't have had a coon dog. I probably would have had a poodle. Roy Blount, Jr., says the reason I've been successful was that I didn't ever want to go back to being poor again.

Was your mother's divorce a problem? You were living in a time and place in which divorce was unusual.

It was a real problem, because the people in the community— church folks—mistreated her, ostracized her. Divorce was just like leprosy back then. But my daddy left us. She didn't ask him to leave. Yet some of the people in the church wouldn't even have anything to do with her because she was a divorced woman.

And I remember when she married my stepdaddy, there was a neighbor who never went to church—a man who would be classified as "pretty tough"—who walked from his house and set a bushel of sweet potatoes on the front porch and said, "I hope y'all are happy. I'm digging my potatoes, and I don't have anything else to give you." I thought it was interesting that a man who never went to church would be one of the few who was nice to my mama.

And then when my mama married my stepdaddy and he was a pillar in the church—especially financially—everything was fine.

Did people treat you differently because of her?

I don't know. They probably talked about me. They probably said, "That's that little old Clower boy. He won't ever amount to nothing, be snatched up by the hair of his head."

I remember after I got out of Mississippi State and went to work for Mississippi Chemical, I called on the late Fred Anderson at

Gloster. His daddy owned a lumber company and he remembered my daddy hauling lumber and driving a truck and the first time I ever called on him was about Christmas time. He said, "Jerry, I want to tell you that I remember how you come up and you've amounted to something. I want to congratulate you." He said, "I want to give you a Christmas present." And he gave me a hundred dollar bill. And as long as he lived—from that day until the day he died—every Christmas he'd give me a hundred dollar bill for "amounting to something."

As a child did you dream of being an entertainer?

No. I dreamed of being a sailor. We would be cutting stove wood and we'd cut the tree down and I would go get up in the top of the tree while it was laying on the ground and stand on the trunk and reach and get limbs and I would play like I was sailing. I would pull the limb on the left to sail to the left and I'd pull the limb on the right to go to the right. I was sailing the high seas.

When I was speaking for Mississippi Chemical, sometimes somebody would come up afterwards and say, "Good gracious, I just went to the national convention and heard Paul Harvey; you're as good as him." Now, I'm not going to lie. Driving back home, I'd say to myself, "You reckon that's right?" So every time I would perform, I'd try to do a little bit better.

Were the Amite County people surprised when you became a star?

I'm sure they were. My mama says I was "longheaded"—a daredevil, one who would take a risk, dive higher out of the sweet gum tree at the swimming hole than anybody else—and a big mouth. Yes, I think they were surprised. But, thank God, I think they are pleased.

Why do you think you've been popular as an entertainer for over twenty years?

Sincerity! People can trust me. They see me on a television show, and they buy a ticket to come and see me in concert. They don't get disappointed and have to get up and run out because I'm different from what I am on television. People like a good ole boy if he's sincere. They love him and come to his shows. I come across as being honest and sincere, and if I recommend something—even a product on television—I done tried it and believe in it.

What do you do that makes people laugh?

I tell about something funny that happened to real folks; and the funniest things in the world actually happened. I don't think I'm necessarily a comic; I think I'm a humorist. A comic tells funny stories, and a humorist tells stories funny.

What is this gift that you have—to take a story and tell it funny? Can you describe it?

No, not really. The story that got me started in show business is the coon huntin' story. I've performed it probably four or five thousand times, but I never perform it that I'm not actually *there* in the middle of the story. I'm under the tree, "Whew, knock him out, John." And I can be John in the tree, and then I can see the dogs get into a fight, "Shoo, dog! Get back. Knock him out, John!" I live it.

A lot of these stories I ought not to have any credit for them—only for the ability to tell what I saw.

How much of what you say is based on fact and how much comes out of your imagination?

My stories are all almost true. In just about everything that I do, something truthful triggered me to do it. I work up some routines that just come to me, that were factual things that happened in my life or someone else's, but I may apply the facts to certain situations which didn't happen actually at all.

Can you give some examples?

I heard about a situation where a church had made up some money and sent a fellow off to learn how to be a preacher. He come back in about two years and said there were some certain portions of the Bible he didn't believe. It just broke all of them's hearts because they had done made up the money for him. When I heard that story, I applied it to East Fork: we made up money and sent an ole boy off to school, and then he got back. I asked my mama—and here's where the imagination comes in—I asked my mama, "Mama, why does he come to church if he don't believe the Bible?"

She said, "Well, son, his mama makes him, and he ain't got no choice if he stays with her."

Well, he come to church one Sunday and we were walking out of church and a little girl walked up to him and said, "Somebody told me you didn't believe all the Bible."

He said, "That's right."

"Well, that's awful."

"I got off to college," he told her, "and I took a biology course and found that a whale's throat ain't big enough to swallow a grapefruit. I just don't believe a big fish swallowed Jonah."

"Well, the Bible says it and I believe it, and that settles it."

Now, if I was in Nashville telling this story, I'd call this fellow "Will," because Will Campbell's a hippy preacher from East Fork now living in Nashville. Then Will would get a kick out of it.

"Well, Brother Will, the Bible says it. I believe it and that settles it."

"Well, I don't reckon we'll ever know, will we?"

The little girl said, "When I get to heaven, I'm going to ask Jonah."

"What if Jonah ain't in heaven?" Brother Will said.

"Well, then *you* can ask him," she said.

I first heard that story and it was true, but then my imagination finished it.

How do you actually put together your stories? Do you write them down or keep them all in your head?

You know, I never sit down and say, "Now look, I've got to plan me a story." It just kind of comes, and when it comes, I'll make a note of it and put it in a box. About a month before I record, I'll get my notes out of that box and review them. I may have the same note in the box five times. I get much of my stuff when I'm riding alone and just thinking about things.

But the creativeness—like in the coon hunt, my number one story—is making things just fit. Like in, "Is that you, Mr. Barron?" and "I had one of them carbide lights that you hang on your cap," and a few little things like that I throw in.

When I do this thing about negativism, for instance, I say, "The most negative human being I've ever known is Clovis Ledbetter. Clovis was so negative he didn't even want to be a Ledbetter. He always wanted to be a log truck." And I'll talk about that: "Clovis wanted to be a log truck. His bread wasn't quite done, and Clovis, at recess, he'd get stuck in a mud hole. Clovis never said a word till he was twenty-two years old. I say, "Y'all know what got Clovis to talking?" Then I put my hand up and get the lights out of my eyes, and I look out into the audience. I say, "Girls. Azlee DeLaughter flung a cravin' on Clovis. The ugliest female girl woman God ever allowed to be birthed in the state of Mississippi. Azlee had to slip up on the dipper to get a drink of water." And then this just comes to me: "If Moses had seen Azlee, we'd a had another commandment. 'Thou shalt not be so ugly.'"

My manager, Tandy Rice, calls that talent. I just call it the Lord blessing you and letting you think things are funny, I reckon.

Talk a little more about the creative process.

If I have any talent, it's the talent to remember. People will come up to me and say, "Jerry, do you remember when we did so-and-so?" I may have forgotten, but then I go back and review it.

Sometimes now I will take an old story and put it in modern day. But the creativeness of it—gosh, as I go along, especially when I'm recording—I come up with some things that's just so far superior to what I had planned to put on the record.

You mean you compose the story as you are telling it?

When I'm recording, I have to have a few notes so I can remember what I want to lay out. When I go to perform to a live audience, though, I just wing it.

I just recorded my twenty-first album at the University of Alabama, and I walked out on stage to finish this album. I said, "You know the most humiliating thing that ever happened to me since I've been a grown adult man happened to me right here at the University of Alabama." Now this is foreign to what I'm planning to do.

And I said, "I was here playing football for Mississippi State years ago, standing on the sidelines on the kick-off team ready to go out to take my position on the field. The cheerleaders were saying, 'Go Bama, Go Bama, Go Bama, Go.' I looked over and a circus-type fellow was leading an elephant right there in front of our bench. The cheerleaders were saying, 'Go Bama, Go Bama, Go Bama, Go.'" And I said, "That elephant *did*." And I described how we reacted to it and all of that.

And when I got through with the show someone said, "Boy, that was a great story you thought up." I said, "So help me God. It didn't come to me until I walked out." But it is a true story. I had forgotten it.

So the creativeness sometimes comes from who you are telling a story to.

When you're in concert with a great crowd of people, can it be personal enough for you to draw inspiration from them?

Sure. Especially if I'm close enough and I can see a few of them. Sometimes I'll be going along and I ain't doing too good. Directly, I'll hit a nerve and I double back and bring some of that in.

At the state fair in Virginia last year, it was kind of a cold night and I didn't see nothing but negativism from people all day. So, when I got up there on stage, I said, "I'm trying to stamp out negativism. Old Dan Rather's been trying to put on a recession on CBS news for about two weeks. Y'all watch him. He comes out there looking like he's just gotten over a hookworm treatment." They yelled, so I knew that they wanted to be cheered up.

This was close to military installations, and there was talk about the war. I just got to talking about "let's stamp out negativism," and we just had a good time. I had never used this approach, but I put some routines about negativism on the next album.

The greatest review I got all last year was at the Virginia State Fair, after the show I just mentioned. I bought the paper the next morning, the Richmond *Times-Dispatch*. It said: "Why should 3,000 people at the state fair sit for nearly an hour on cold bleachers listening to a former fertilizer salesman talk about Yazoo City, Mississippi? When I was about ten watching 'Nashville on the Road' and Jerry Clower came on, I used to change the channel. The loudmouth, unsophisticated, cloddish comedian was the most obnoxious television personality I had ever been exposed to."

As I'm reading this, I'm just sinking. But I keep on reading: "All that changed at the state fair last night as I listened spellbound to every word this southern humorist had to say and laughed aloud with fans of his from years gone by . . . *Clower Power*! We love you too, Jerry!"

Do audiences outside the South always understand your stories?

Yes, but sometimes I have to help them out. When I played theater-in-the-round in Boston, Massachusetts, I told the coon huntin' story. Now, if I had been in Lafayette, Louisiana, I would have just said "coon huntin'" and gone on with the story. But in Boston when I said "coon huntin'," I went on to explain: "We take a group of hound dogs that's bred specifically to smell the scent of a raccoon. We turn them loose in the woods, and they start sniffing on the ground. And if they can smell where the raccoon walked, they can track him and bark. If they get close enough, they run him up a tree." Then I went on with the story, and they laughed in Boston at coon huntin' just like they laugh in Raleigh or Mobile or Richmond.

I remember years ago I saw my friend Justin Wilson on the "Ed Sullivan Show." He told a story about a Cajun: the Cajun got into a *pirogue* and went to town. Well, if he had defined *pirogue* right there, it would have been a hilariously funny story. But when he got to the punch line, not a soul said a word—not even Ed Sullivan. They didn't understand the point, and I never felt so sorry for him in all my life. If he had said, "A Cajun got a *pirogue*—which is similar to an Indian canoe—and paddled himself into the bayou town," then went on, they all would have laughed.

It works the other way around, too. When I performed in Boston, Massachusetts, they said, "Put your hands together. Theater-in-the-round welcomes Merle Haggard and Jerry Clower to the land of the bean and the cod." If my mama had been there, she'd have slapped him. When us good old boys were growing up, "cod" was an expression for testicles. And here I am in Boston, and the man says, "Welcome to the land of the bean and the cod."

I tell this on stage in the South sometimes. Well, you can see some of the good old boys kind of laugh because they don't want their wife to know they know something she don't know. And then I stop and I say, "Cod in Boston is a fish. And they eat it with their beans." Fine. I ain't trying to change that tradition.

Of course, there's a lot of regional tradition that's national tradition now. People all over the country know more about the South today because of the Nashville Network and because country music has gotten so far. And there's not enough credit given to "Hee Haw"—that show really blowed the world asunder. There's no more North, South, East, and West as we once knew it.

Have you ever had any hostile audiences?

I have never had a hostile audience. I have been concerned after I'd go four or five minutes when I didn't think they were with me like they ought to be. I would name off the Ledbetters—Ardell, Burnell, Raynell, W. L., Lanell, Odell, Udell, Marcel, Claude, Eugene, and

Clovis; and if I got more reaction from one of them than I did the other, I would double back and put him in the next routine.

The closest I ever come to having a hostile audience—which wasn't their fault—was January 16, 1991, in Richmond, Virginia. I was at a Virginia Turf-Lawn Association convention at the Marriott Hotel. About 800 people were at this convention—these people who would landscape golf courses. And they was *my* kind of folks because they used fertilizer, and I'm an old ex-fertilizer salesman.

I'm sittin' backstage. They finished up with the dinner, and I saw four or five people ease into the auditorium and whisper to someone at a table. I saw whatever message they gave sweep that audience. It come all the way up to the stage. A guy got up and come backstage and said, "They're bombing Iraq. We just went to war. We just went to war. They're bombing them."

And just then, the announcer said, "Now, ladies and gentleman: MCA recording artist, with twenty-one albums on MCA, twelve times Country Comic of the Year, writer of three books, and co-host of 'Country Crossroads,' the largest syndicated radio show in the world—put your hands together and welcome Grand Ole Opry star, Jerry Clower."

The closer I got to the microphone, the madder I got at Saddam Hussein, and the adrenalin started flowing. I said to myself, I'm going to get this audience. I'm going to snatch them up. I've got to get them with me. The adrenalin started flowing just like a Holstein cow standing in the milk barn and she hears that milking machine come on. Well, sometimes milk will go to dripping out of her udder before you can get the milking machine on her. My adrenalin gets to flowing, and it's like a good coon dog that is trailing a coon and all of a sudden he sees him. And I let my milk down.

I hit the audience with every fiber of my being. I hollered and kicked and I got them with me. They got to laughing and right in the middle of the performance I said, "Ladies and gentlemen, at age seventeen I caught the Panama Limited out of McComb, Mississippi, and went off and fought a war on an aircraft carrier. That's why I love this country so much. I know what it took to keep it free. I earned three battle stars and the presidential unit citation for bravery before I was nineteen years of age.

"I know where your mind is right now. I know y'all thinking about the war. They're bombing Iraq. I know you know that. But I don't think it would be a salute to our brave men and women if we called off our show. If you took a vote over there, they'd say, 'Don't let Saddam Hussein rob y'all of the blessing of having a good time. That's what he wants to do.'"

I said, "He ain't going to keep me from doing nothing that I want to do. The armed services is fixing to whip him and we're going to whip him here tonight. I never been prouder to be an American."

Well, they jumped up—about half of them—and went to "high-fiving" and kicking chairs. It was one of the greatest performances I've ever given. And I was received as well as for any performance I ever done.

You seem to have such fun entertaining. Is there any point at which this is hard work?

The constant pulling and shoving and pushing when you're out in the public is hard work. An airplane's late and you get off of one and you got to get to another concourse and three or four people say, "Mr. Clower. You are Jerry Clower. I saw you on television. We want to get our picture made with you."

Well, it's hard work to say, "Darling, I'm about to miss a plane and I don't have time." But sometimes I'd rather miss the flight than for people to talk ugly about me. I do try to make myself available, but some people are so ugly they think I belong to them. They just snatch me around.

Being on stage is the easiest thing I do. Getting to the next place is the hardest.

So, being a celebrity is hard work?

I stopped at a Cracker Barrel a few months ago in Athens, Alabama, and it was four degrees outside. I'd been on a diet, and I got to feeling sorry for myself. I said, "I see a Cracker Barrel and I'm going to go over there and get me some of that country ham." I went over to the Cracker Barrel and signed thirty-nine menus. I never did get to eat because my gravy got cold. Now *that's* hard work to me. I finally went by a Seven-Eleven and got me some Vienna sausages and some crackers.

I'm not complaining about it. I wouldn't be selling the records if I didn't do that. But, boy, sometimes when I get to do a rodeo seven or eight days in a row and I don't have to travel and can stay in the same hotel, I can't wait to get out there and entertain the folks. It's a challenge to me because I love to see people laugh, and laugh together.

Is it ever lonely on the road?

It is lonely on the road, but sometimes you really look forward to the loneliness of the hotel room where you ain't got to talk. You just sit there and think about your grandchildren.

As an entertainer who can create stories as you perform them, what do you think of the writers in your business?

Writers, in my opinion, are the most important part of the show business scene—people who write books, and people who write songs, and people who write plays, and people who write other things in our business.

The great writer of songs and books, Tom T. Hall, said:

> Old dogs care about you
>   even when you make mistakes.
> God bless little children
>   while they're still too young to hate.

That line really done something for me because children are not born bigots. They are trained to be bigots. It grieves my heart to

know that any human being would have a precious child and teach
that child to hate. Tom T. Hall said, "Little children are still too
young to hate," and "Ain't but three things in this world that's
worth a solitary dime: old dogs and children and watermelon wine."

And there's that great song performed by George Jones and written by Bobby Braddock and Curly Putman. I remember the first
time I heard it:

> He said, "I'll love you til I die."
> > She told him, "You'll forget in time."
> As the years went slowly by,
> > she still preyed upon his mind.
> He kept her picture on his wall
> > and went half-crazy now and then.
> But he still loved her through it all.
> He kept some letters by his bed,
> > dated nineteen-sixty-two;
> He had underlined in red
> > every single "I love you";

Well, that's done set me up. I'm driving my car and I'm hearing
this song. Good gracious, that old boy loved her. Ain't that something! He loves her and in the next verse, with about twenty new
fiddles added, Possum Jones—George Jones, the greatest country
singer God ever allowed to be birthed in the world—said, "He
stopped loving her today." Well, I thought I was going to have to
stop my car. Hey, he can't stop loving her: she preyed on his mind.
He went half crazy now and then, put her picture on the wall,
underlined "I love you." He *can't* stop loving her. The song
continued:

> I went to see him just today,
> > but I didn't see no tears;
> All dressed up to go away.
> First time I'd seen him smile in years.

> He stopped loving her today.
> They placed a wreath upon his door.
> And soon they'll carry him away;
>   he stopped loving her today.

I said, "Uh, huh. All right, I feel better now, Possum, because you done set me up that he really loved her and the only way he'd stop loving her was to die."

And ole Possum said,

> She came to see him one last time.
> We all wondered if she would.
> And kept running through our mind,
> This time he's over her for good.

So that's an illustration of great writers. To me, the most talented people in our business are the writers.

And this sort of thing inspires your own stories?

Sure. Yes, sir. Mel Tillis writing songs like "Detroit City, I want to go home." Hey, I done been on a troop train passing not far from Detroit City, and I wanted to go home. And there's other songs. You take Paul Overstreet, the Mississippi boy that's been picked as the number one song writer for four consecutive years—he's written some classics.

To me, the most talented people in our business are the writers. Writers inspire me, and I don't think they get enough credit. You tell any superstar, "You sure are great. You sure can sing pretty." He'll say, "I ain't no better than the song." You've got to have a song.

Chick Dougherty, from MCA records in Nashville, said, "They ain't never been a hit that there wasn't something in the groove that people wanted to hear." I agree with that. I agree with that wholeheartedly.

That goes for your stories, too—like the coon hunt?

WWL, New Orleans, and WBAP, Fort Worth, and WHO, Des Moines, and WWVA, Wheeling, and WSM, Nashville all played the coon hunt. And WABC, I believe it was, and thousands of smaller ones. But when the coon hunt story and the truckers got together: "Hey, good buddy, you heard about the man up in the tree?" Well, it went to number five in the nation in *Billboard*.

So, Chick said, "I don't care how much they played it; if folks didn't respond to it, then there ain't nothing in the groove."

Mississippi has had quite a few literary hits, as well. Do you feel any kinship with your fellow Mississippians who write books?

Now, I respect Mississippi authors—authors like Willie Morris. Willie was a Rhodes Scholar, but he can still write about baseball and dogs. Even good ole boys like him. I went to do the "David Frost Show" in New York City when I first backed into show business. They said, "Yazoo City. Willie Morris—he's editor of *Harper's* Magazine—is from there." I said, "Yes."

And William Faulkner. One day I was with Bennett Cerf and he said, "Well, you're from Mississippi. I did some publishing for William Faulkner."

I said, "Well, I used to sit and drink coffee with him talking about possum huntin'." I thought the man was going to faint. I know he thought I was lying, that a man that talked like I did was not cultured enough to talk with William Faulkner.

I don't think you are lying. How did you come to meet William Faulkner?

I finished Mississippi State in January of 1951 and I got a job as assistant county agent in Oxford, Mississippi, and I was excited. By March of that same year, I was in charge of the 4-H Club work. I hadn't been there very long when they asked me to be the announcer at a local horse show. Before the horse show started, some of the officials were standing around and somebody whispered, "There comes William Faulkner."

I said, "Which one is Mr. Faulkner?"

Mrs. Lowe, who was the mother of some twins that had starred in the movie made in Oxford of Faulkner's novel, *Intruder in the Dust*, leaned over and said, "Jerry, he's the one that looks like he just fought a wasp nest with his hat."

Well, there he come, with little patches on his elbows, his tweed coat and his tweed hat, and a little pipe in his mouth.

I wasn't in awe of him until I had the privilege of sitting at the College Inn and the Mansion restaurant in Oxford on occasions and drinking coffee and talking to William Faulkner. I remember there was a fellow named Big John Cullen, who was one of William Faulkner's good ole boy running mates. I was most impressed that here was an academically excellent world-famous man, William Faulkner, but yet—and this is why I respect him—he could talk about country things.

I remember one morning in the College Inn, John Cullen told Faulkner that there was too many rabbits being killed on the Batesville-Oxford Highway. He thought that Faulkner ought to go before the state legislature and get them to build a rabbit-proof fence, because if times got hard, we'd need to eat them rabbits.

I remember that when William Faulkner went to Sweden to accept the Nobel Prize, John Cullen wrote to the king of Sweden, King Gustav, and told him that his best friend was coming over there, and that he was a literary giant. He wanted Gustav to know that while Faulkner was over there, he couldn't do no better thing than to feed him some 'possum and collards. We all got extremely excited when the king of Sweden wrote John Cullen back.

Aren't you a friend of Will Campbell's, the author who wrote Brother to a Dragonfly *and other books?*

Will Davis Campbell lived about a mile from where I was born. I never remember a day in my life I didn't know Will Davis Campbell.

Will Davis is a graduate of Yale. He was thirty years ahead of his time on how to treat black people, but he can describe in detail how to make molasses, clean chitterlings, or sharpen a hoe.

Will Davis Campbell taught me how to tie a tie. I didn't know how to tie a tie. I remember he tied it and showed me, and he said it was the new Windsor knot. I don't wear ties now—just simply on rare occasions; but when I do wear one, I tie it just like Will showed me.

I remember when me and Will Davis and Paul, Will's younger brother who was more my age, was going to a peanut boiling down south of East Fork. There used to be a spring that run across the road all the time; it left water in the road. Just as we eased through that spring running across that road, the battery fell out of a '38 Ford that Will Davis was driving. Well, me and Paul said, "We've had it."

We wasn't as smart as Will Davis. What we was going to do was just walk somewhere and say, "Can you get a rope and come pull us?"

Will Davis got that brain going. He said, "Now, wait a minute, boys. Jerry, you strip off and give me your clothes. Get naked and crawl under this '38 Ford. The battery's just fell down and hit the ground. You get your hands under that battery and push it up. Now, you're going to be muddy and wet. Push the battery up and hold it. I'm getting a piece of barbed wire off the fence over there, and when you push it up, I'm going to tie it."

Well, we did that, and it worked. Then I stepped off in a little creek and washed all the sand and the mud off of me and shook myself like a wet dog. Will handed me my clothes back a piece at a time, and I redressed and we went on to the peanut boiling just like nothing happened.

Have you ever met Eudora Welty?

Yes. One afternoon I had to take my daughter Katy to a voice lesson near the Belhaven campus. I had about 45 minutes to kill, and I was just driving around in the neighborhood. I looked down the street and there was a television truck with all the wires running out of it and into a house. Well, my curiosity got the best of me, and I just followed those wires inside to where the lights and cameras and people were. Just as I got inside the door, I heard a voice say, "Mr. Clower, come right in." It was Miss Eudora Welty, and the BBC was producing a program about her.

Did you know any other Mississippi writers or artists?

When I lived in Oxford, Mississippi, I had an apartment with Miss Theora Hamblett. Me and Homerline moved in with her in a house with some college students. A long hall come down the middle of the house; Miss Hamblett lived over on one side and me and Homerline lived on the other one. I remember she was dabbling with some little old painting. I kind of made fun of it to some students who lived upstairs. I said, "That stump out in the middle of a field ain't nothing."

Homerline kept telling me, "Jerry, that lady's enjoying that. Quit telling her that you think her pictures are nothing." I think the one I criticized is hanging in the Chase Manhattan Bank in New York City.

She was a wonderful, wonderful lady. My wife just loved her, and we have fond memories of living in the house with Miss Theora Hamblett. Little did we know that one day she'd be a famous picture painter, and I'd have twenty-one albums on MCA Records and be writing a book for the University Press of Mississippi!

Did you ever meet Elvis Presley?

No, but I sent him some word and he sent me some word. We knew one another and about one another. T.G. Shepard had it arranged that me and Elvis and him was going to set down on the floor and talk all night. Elvis died just before I had an opportunity to do that.

I wish people would quit saying that Elvis was alive. J.D. Sumner—the world's greatest bass singer, who now performs as J.D. Sumner and the Stamps Quartet—was in charge of Elvis' funeral. He saw him embalmed. He put the concrete on him. I wish these people who keep saying Elvis is alive would talk to J.D. Sumner and find out the truth.

Besides the Bible, do you have any favorite books?

Yes, the books of Louis L'Amour. I read every book he's ever written, and I love the Sacketts. They come out of the Clinch Mountains of Tennessee and headed west. Everywhere they went they had to use the gun, sometimes to carry out the philosophy of the Sacketts, which was to be good neighbors. But they never shot nobody that didn't need shooting. I've always checked it.

And when I was a kid I had an English teacher, Mrs. Ray J. Turner. She lives in Hamburg, Mississippi. I love her because she got me to read *Ivanhoe* and other books. I read *Ivanhoe* and then she put me on *Tap Roots* and *Oh Promised Land* by James Street.

Then several years ago, I saw Charlie Daniels, my show business buddy, and he was giving a "promo" asking people to read Louis L'Amour books. Well, I respect and love Charlie Daniels so much I just bought a paperback to read on the airplane. Now I have all of his books in my library in my house. He didn't just write Westerns; he was a brilliant fellow.

What are some major forces that influenced you both as a person and as a humorist?

Well, the greatest influence on my life has been Christianity.

My mother took me to the old East Fork Baptist Church, and at age thirteen I publicly professed my faith, and was baptized in the Amite River—me and my wife together. I have grown up in the church, and I do try to use the Bible as a guide book on what I do; and we've been successful doing that. Ninety percent of all of my social life is in the local church.

Now, what I'm saying is not very popular, but what I'm saying happens to be truth. I think in this day and time being very religious is coming under attack, and people are brushing it off more than any other time in my life.

I was watching the "Phil Donahue" show not too long ago and one of his guests said, "Phil, I've had an experience with the Lord. I've been born again and I've gotten into a church. It's the power of God that I can change my lifestyle, and I want to because it doesn't fit in with all my parents' thoughts."

Donahue's answer was, "Ha, ha, ha," just right up in his face. That's the ultimate put-down of anybody. It really shocked me that he who claims to be so tolerant would be so intolerant: he laughed in the man's face.

But the other side of this is that if the young man had said, "Well, I met a friend who told me how you could set spread-legged on the beach an hour before sunrise as the sun come up. If you didn't blink your eyes for the next thirty minutes and you was able to concentrate fully on the little waves bubbling over your crotch as you set on the seashore, then if you could sustain, you could change your lifestyle. Donahue would probably have said, "Tell me more. Wonderful. Isn't that a beautiful thing?"

Do you attribute your happy marriage to the fact that you and Homerline are in the church together?

The greatest thing that ever happened to me was when I became a Christian. Now I believe that. My Christian faith comes first in my life.

I remember seeing Homerline first at church. I thought she was the prettiest thing ever I'd seen in all my life. Then we had a revival meeting and I worked it around to where I could sit by her and hold her hymn book. The Thursday night of the revival, when the pastor gave the invitation, I walked down the aisle, and Reverend Price Brock (who was pastor of the Baptist church in Pickens, Mississippi, up until his retirement) dealt with me and I sat down and he reached to take the hand of someone else. This little blonde-headed girl that I had been sittin' with followed me down the aisle.

So, we both made our decisions the same night. We walked down the aisle of an old country church together on a Thursday night

following the fourth Sunday in July when we have dinner-on-
the-grounds. The next Sunday we were baptized in the Amite
River. Walked up out of the water together. I never dated another
girl. I never had another sweetheart. We've been happily married
for forty-four years. And as I speak to you, after forty-four years of
married life, my wife is chairman of the Pulpit Search Committee for the same old church that we grew up in and is fixing to
recommend a preacher next Sunday to the congregation for us to
vote on.

And this is East Fork Baptist Church?

East Fork Baptist Church. It's on the east prong of Amite River.
The Amite River comes down through Amite County; and up in the
northern part it forks. The east fork runs east of Liberty, and the
west fork runs west of Liberty. That church was organized in 1810.
They've been having dinner-on-the-grounds the fourth Sunday in
July since 1810. So, I come from a fine heritage. I really do.

From the moment my stepfather married my mama in the house
where I grew up, we had some rules and we had some laws. You
break the rules, they'd talk to you. You break the law, you was
punished. One of the laws was you didn't get up on Sunday morning
and ask, "Are we going to church today?" It was just automatic. So,
I was carried to church. (Now that's a good southern word—"carried." And it bothers some of my Yankee friends, cause they think
my mama actually picked me up and toted me to East Fork
church.)

I just grew up in the church, and I continued to go. It's worked for
me and my family.

Why do you love the Baptist church so?

I love the Baptist church because they ministered to me and, in my
opinion, told me the truth about the Bible and salvation. I had that
"experience of grace" that only comes from the saving power of

God. I love the Baptist church now because it's one of the few democracies left on earth. As an illustration, I was presiding at the business meeting the other night. (I am chairman of the deacons in our church.) A young man on the back row asks, "Could we vote in this business meeting to have a secret ballot?"

I said, "Yes sir."

He asks, "Well, what if the church by-laws say that you can't vote by secret ballot?"

I said, "We can change the by-laws here tonight if you want to. All it takes is fifty percent plus one. And if you can get the votes, you can tear the church down or move it."

We have discussion and everybody discusses, and the pastor's vote is equal to the youngest member in the congregation. Everybody has the same vote. So, that's one reason I love the Baptist church. I think it is a true democracy, and I believe in democracy. I don't believe in dictatorship.

You have been outspoken about your belief in racial equality and integration. How did you arrive at your beliefs?

Well, it first started when I was about twelve years old. I remember being in Sunday school, and the night before I knew a group of men had took a man out and whipped him. Took a *black* man out of his house and "straightened him out"—whipped him. I remember that morning in Sunday school the teacher saying, "Beware of women who paint their lips and wear short dresses and smoke them ole ready-rolled cigarettes." (I reckon if you rolled your own, it was better because that showed a sign of you being thrifty. See, ready-rolls was then extravagant because it took a lot more money to buy ready-rolled than it did to roll your own.) I had heard that "God's grace is sufficient. If God be for us, who can be against us."

"Any questions?" she asked.

I said, "Yessum. What about the beating they gave the man last night?"

The teacher put her finger in my face and said, "Don't you ever bring that up in this church again. There are just some things that you don't discuss."

Well, I got confused. I'm real confused because she just said, "God's grace is sufficient." We sang, "Take your burdens to the Lord and leave them there." I had a burden, but I was learning that there are certain burdens that you didn't bring up in the church. So, I got confused. Why could God deal with all this other stuff and why could he make the heavens and earth, but when I needed some guidance on who to love or who to hate, His grace wasn't sufficient?

The most spiritual person I knew when I was a little boy—that I just would have wanted to grow up to love God as much as she did— told us children that there'd be a black heaven and a white heaven. She believed the Bible. And people looked to her and called her for spiritual guidance.

After I become a Christian, my convictions got to pricking my conscience. I couldn't live with some of the things that I had been taught and be a maximum Christian. I would have to compromise with the Christian convictions if I believed some things that I had been taught as a child.

Even though some of those things had been taught to you by Christians?

Yes, sure, people who claimed to be Christians. When you grow up in a segregated society, it is a way of life. Southern tradition runs so deep, and hatred has penetrated us so strong, we southerners wouldn't even let God straighten it out in our lives. I lived with that, and that's the only thing that I knew until I got to asking questions.

When did you first begin to ask questions?

When I joined the navy and went to Williamsburg, Virginia, to Camp Perry. I was sittin' on a bunk in the barracks talking to a

Polish guy from New York. Then somebody come up and said, "Look at them damn kikes."

I'm seventeen years old. I had never been away from home. I said, "Look at what?"

He said, "Them damn kikes. Don't you see them?"

I said, "What are you talking about?"

He said, "Them Jews. Look there—they are identical twins coming in the barracks."

I said, "How can you tell they're Jews?"

He just said, "Ha, ha, ha. The rebel don't know what a Jew is."

Well, that was my first introduction to the fact that some folks was prejudiced against people other *than* blacks. I was furious that he would criticize a *white* man—just furious and ready to fight that he didn't like him. I assumed we had enough blacks to hate. And where I was from, you was either black or white, period. If I knew a Jew, I didn't know it. I knew some Lebanese. But I didn't not like *them* because they was *white*. I felt a little bit better about my bigotry: at least I didn't hate *white* people.

But then they would tell me that blacks was as good as me. I near about come to blows because I was taught different than that.

Then, as I got through the service and under battle situations, you didn't care whether they was green, blue, black, or white. You was all trying to protect your life.

Did your attitude toward black people change when you were in the navy?

No, I was a while making the change. I remember when that woman, Rosa Parks, was trying to ride on that bus in Montgomery: "What does she mean doing that? Boy, I'll tell you what I would do if I was over there!" And then I got to thinking one day, Jerry, you're a Christian. What difference does it make where somebody sits on a cotton-picking bus?

I was in Birmingham selling fertilizer right after they bombed that church. They'd bombed and killed three precious little black children. The following Monday I was driving through Birmingham, and I had the radio on and the guy was a disc jockey—he was black—and he was trying to rally all the black children. "Just say, *I'm somebody!* Right now I know it's hard. They've bombed and killed you, but just stop right now and say, 'I'm somebody.' "

I stopped at a red light by a school bus, and a little black boy was looking out the window at me. I let the window down and I said, "I know you are somebody, son, and if I could get this scoundrel that bombed you just because you're black, I would."

Because of deals like these, my Christian convictions got to pricking my conscience.

No black could travel across the state of Mississippi, eat, or use the bathroom. There was no place for them to use the bathroom, and if they stopped on the side of the road, they would be shot for indecent exposure. That bothered me. So, gradually my Christian convictions got to pricking my conscience, and then the court ordered integration of the schools. I sat down with my kids and I said, "Well, let's discuss this."

We are talking now about 1970?

Yes. And we got to discussing it. All my children got together, and my son Ray asked me about a young man that he went to public schools with. He said, "Daddy, can he go to the new private academy they are building?"

I said, "No."

He said, "Well, he made the highest grade on the ACT test ever made in this county. Man, Howard University and some of them big universities are bidding on him—just like trying to bid to buy a mule—to get his brain in their school. He's president of the student body here in the public school. His daddy ginned several thousand bales of cotton. He is qualified academically. He's got the money. Why couldn't he go?"

I said, "'Cause he's black."

My son gave me a new definition of bigotry. He said, "Well, Daddy, that's the only thing we've brought up so far that he ain't got no control over. Now if he had the choice of picking his mama and daddy and he still preferred to be black, it wouldn't bother me as bad because he chose to get into a race that is discriminated against. But he didn't pick his mama and daddy. And to tell him he can't go to that school just 'cause he's black—I ain't going over there. I'm going to stay in the public school."

Well, some people get furious when you bring it up now. "Why have you got to bring that up?" Why did they ever do it? *Why did they ever do it?*

Your friend Will Campbell who was an early white civil rights activist in Mississippi—did he have any influence on your change of attitude?

I remember when he was ordained to be preacher at the East Fork Baptist Church. I remember how his old godly granddaddy, Uncle Bunt Campbell, put his hands on Will's head to ordain him—inasmuch as Uncle Bunt was a deacon and that was his calling to put his hands on Will's head. I remember how Uncle Bunt rested his forehead on the top of his hands, and he stayed there a long time 'cause that was his grandson.

Then Will went off and got educated and got to advocating some things about racial inequality. My Christian convictions hadn't pricked my conscience enough yet, and I fussed at Will. Why in the world would he leave Amite County, Mississippi, and go off up to the University of Mississippi and do some of the things he was advocating?

I wrote him a letter. I was real brilliant the way I phrased my letter. I said that it bothered me that him and other preachers had decided to change their minds about the calling of God only after the Supreme Court said some of the things that they were advocating was illegal. I said, "If God called you to be a preacher and you think we ought to have been doing some things for blacks, why didn't you preach it before the Supreme Court made their decision? As powerful as the Holy Spirit is, looks like some preacher would have stood up and done this on his own without the Supreme Court saying, 'We need to do this.'" Well, Will didn't answer my letter.

Years later, I went to see him and hugged him. (And he's still a little too liberal for me on some subjects, but that don't keep us from having Christian fellowship. He's my wife's blood first cousin. I love Brother Will.) And I asked him what about that letter.

He said, "I read that letter and turned to my wife and said, 'Old Jerry's made out of the right stuff. He'll come around, and one of these days he'll tell me he's sorry he wrote the letter.'" And he was right.

He was just as right as he could be.

When was the first time you expressed yourself openly about race?

About 1969 or 1970, when the schools were desegregated. Because it took me that long to gradually get changed to where I *could* express myself. And you know, many couldn't express themselves then. They'd get fired. If I had not worked for Owen Cooper, I couldn't have expressed myself in 1969 and 1970. I saw preachers who couldn't preach against segregation because they'd be thrown out of their pulpit.

People will say, "Oh, Jerry, it wasn't that bad."

I'd say, "Don't tell me. I saw them fire a preacher because his wife just *taught* in the public schools."

They said, "Jerry, don't tell that."

I said, "Don't tell me, I paid his way to Utah. He didn't have a job. I gave him money to move to Utah and get a job out there."

Somebody asked my Yazoo City friend, Charles Jackson, one time, "Why in the world does Jerry say these things about race?"

Charles said, "Jerry has done got so rich, he ain't scared no more."

But the truth of the matter was I worked for a man who would let me express myself—a man who believed *all* of the Bible, who *didn't* say, "Lord, I believe everything you tell me, but I still hate blacks." There was a lot of people who felt like I did that couldn't say a word because they'd get fired from their jobs.

But, hallelujah! It's just like night and day now compared to that. A lot of the difference is because the law *makes* us do it. I want people to integrate, especially those that claim to be Christians, because it's *right* to do it. Now, the other side of it is, after I stuck my neck out, they threatened to burn my house and said, "You nigger-lover."

This was in Yazoo City?

Yes, and even children in Sunday school called my children nigger-lovers because they went to what had been a Negro school.

When Mississippi State got integrated, they hadn't been up there very long till the blacks went before the president and wanted a black dormitory. And then I see where they are going to get a black supervisors' association, and I saw the other day where, in the *Dawg's Bite* at Mississippi State, they are going to have a Mississippi State Black Students' Association now. And I cannot fathom their dumbness in doing this. I'm opposed to black caucuses. They don't have no Italian caucus or Polish caucus. "Well, Jerry, we've been discriminated against for so long, we need this." I doubt it. You've got radicals on both sides.

I wish that we could see a census and a redistricting when we are so harmonious they'll say, "Districted according to people bodies." *Bodies*—make sure that you have it correct. You've got as many bodies in this district as you do in that one. And you don't ever say *minority*. You don't ever say whites. You don't ever say blacks. Or any other group.

Just people?

People. And we can do that, and the Bible Belt ought to have done it before anybody else. But we didn't have our theology right about the word of God. The white supremacists want to use the Bible about who Cain married to say that the blacks are under a curse and that kind of mess.

But if Southern Baptists ever, as a whole, get their theology right about "Whosoever will, may come" and "Anybody that God made, don't you call them unclean," we will have come a long way. The Bible says it, and it's real simple.

Do you mean white Baptists opening their church doors to blacks?

I ain't talking about proselytizing. I ain't talking about going out and breaking up black churches. I just mean, "Whosoever will, may come." If y'all want to come, come. If y'all think we're too sophisticated, then get in one where they clap their hands and holler. If ours ain't sophisticated enough, stay in one that is. But we ain't going to push you off the steps.

I remember when you spoke to a Jackson civic club and said something like, "Anybody who thinks black people are treated as well as white people ought to be black for one day."

Well, I said, "If you think that we have equality, then you'd better thank God you're white." I got a lot of criticism. I gave an illustration about when Mississippi College was fixing to come and sing in the First Baptist Church of Yazoo City. The choir director at Mississippi College called the pastor and said, "Hey, since you invited us, we have now got one black in the choir."

So, the pastor of our church didn't even think about it. He said, "That will be fine; just come right on." But he brought it up to the deacons, and two of them started telephone calling. They forced it to a Sunday morning vote on whether that black could come and sing in our church or not. It passed about eighty percent to let him come.

But I said, "That proves there's not one drop of Jerry Clower in God. He is an omnipotent, wonderful, fair God because if there was one drop of Jerry Clower in God, everybody in that church who voted against that boy would be turned jet black. I'd have me a system set up at the back of the church like they've got at the airport—a security system. If you come to church bragging about you're a Christian and you love Jesus, when you walk through the 'God machine,' it would detect whether you hate blacks. If you were a bigot, the minute you got through that machine, you'd be black as Pearl Bailey." That's what I said. And that's what got a lot of them mad.

I don't want to throw away all of my common sense. I'm proud of Mississippi. I remember years ago I was doing the Iowa State Fair, and an old boy said, "Mr. Clower, how does it feel being from a racist state?"

I said, "Well, it's very obvious you're at your best when you ain't inhibited by no facts."

I said, "Let me tell you what the facts are." Bill Waller and somebody had just put Jimmy Swan out of the first primary in the governor's race; I used that as an illustration. Well, here was a bigot running against two racial liberals and the bigot lost.

But it's still a mystery to me how godly people can tithe their income, give to the poor, read the Bible, pray, love folks, and let God run every fiber of their being except how they treat black people. But why does racism run so deep? I just can't fathom it. I don't have any idea. I don't know. Does it make any difference where anybody sets on a durn bus?

What do you think is the future of race relations in Mississippi?

I think they're going to get better. But we are going to have to quit seeing who can pop off to the press to criticize the other one the most.

There is no limit to what can be done if it doesn't matter who gets the credit. If we could just get a few people to take that attitude, there is no limit to what can be done.

The late Mr. M.B. Swayze, who ran the Mississippi Economic

Council from Yazoo County, told me one time, "Jerry, you can't give away credit. It may take it a long time to catch up, but eventually who ought to have the credit will get it."

And we need some leadership in this state. All we've needed all along was some leadership. And that's all we need now—leadership. Do you know that an ole Mississippi boy, if he's led properly, will do the right thing about ninety-nine percent of the time.

If you could invite to dinner at your house on Amazing Grace Lane any ten people who live now or have ever lived and could sit and talk to them, whom would you invite?

I'd invite Leontyne Price because I respect her so much. She's got to be the world's foremost high note singer that could rare back and do it. I've heard her sing. Didn't understand nothing she said, but I knew the best there was, was doing it, and chill bumps come up and down my spine.

She never knocked where she come from. She come back to Laurel, Mississippi, and her mother would be the maid to serve the little hors d'oeuvres and the punch. One of them who was there told me that Leontyne got an apron and tied it around herself and helped her mama serve. There she was revered all over the world as a great singer. I want Leontyne Price to be there.

And General Patton. That'd be a great contrast, but I'd like to ask him a few questions. He did some things that nobody ever done, good and bad, in military circles. I'd like to talk to him. I would also like very much for President Truman and General Douglas MacArthur to eat with me.

I would want Billy Graham there, and I would like John Wesley to be there. I was driving through Savannah with a friend who pointed out a church and said, "John Wesley used to be pastor of that church." I said, "Stop." I went in there and I felt a tingling all over. Here's a man that put one foot on Europe and one foot on the United States and preached and started Methodism. I would want him there with me. Billy Graham and John Wesley.

And I'd want Bo Diddley, the rhythm and blues singer who grew up out from McComb, Mississippi. He doesn't mind getting on TV with Larry King and saying that parents need to be more responsible. That's an old cliché, and people keep saying that, but it's true. If you have children, you ought to be committed to try and take care of them. You birthed them.

And Dr. George Washington Carver. He did the best he could with what he had, and he done it "now."

I'd want to have Tandy Rice there because he's my manager and has directed my show business career all these years. Talking about traditional values, we've operated on a handshake all these years. If my granddaddy had a problem with a neighbor and you asked him, "Who is your lawyer?" he wouldn't have known what you was talking about. Tandy and I have operated that way, too. I would want Tandy to eat with us so we could talk about it.

I probably would go back and pick some ole boy who was on that aircraft carrier with me in the South Pacific, that was as scared as I was when the chaplain would get on the PA system and say, "There is a kamikaze diving on the *Bennington*." I'd probably pick that ole boy from Georgia that said, "Clower, don't worry about it; if they kill us, they can't eat us."

My last choices would probably be Roy Rogers and Dale Evans, because when I went overseas and stopped at the Hollywood canteen, they put on a program for us. They come out singing "Don't Fence Me In." I've met Dale Evans several times and been on shows with her, but I've never set and just talked to Brother Roy. I would like to talk to him.

That's more than ten, but I want two more. I would love to have the original Zorro, whoever was Zorro—I would love to feed him. And I would love to have the real Robin Hood at the table with me to talk about Little John and all of them. It would just be fabulous. I would love that. First picture show I remember seeing was Robin Hood, and the next one was Zorro.

Me and my buddy, Marcel Ledbetter, went out in Amite County

and put a Z on every corn crib door in the fourth district. We loved Zorro and hitchhiked to McComb, Mississippi, not long after that. A Catholic nun was crossing the street when Marcel run and took her by the elbow and helped her across the street. She said, "Young man, thank you so much. You have such good manners." And Marcel said, "Any friend of Zorro is a friend of mine."

I know you think that loyalty is important. Can you tell me why?

If you're not loyal, you're not *nothing*. I heard a talk show the other day, and a member of the Mississippi legislature, when the host got to criticizing the legislature, said, "I'm not here to defend the legislature." Well, he ought to resign. Criticize the Grand Ole Opry to me, and I'll show you how to be loyal. Criticize my church. Criticize MCA records. Criticize my agent, Tandy Rice. Criticize Mississippi Chemical. Criticize my friends. Criticize my bank. I'll take up for them. I'm loyal to them. If I can't be loyal to them, I'll change my method of operation.

I've seen Mr. Owen Cooper, a man I loved, and the greatest, smartest human being I've ever known, near about run out of gas one time when we were driving from Tennessee into Mississippi. I said, "Mr. Cooper, you're out of gas."

He said, "I'm trying to make it back to Mississippi because my state will get several cents a gallon." I've had good training. I buy at home. I trade cars at home.

I buy cars made in the United States of America. If that's bad, it's just bad. I'm loyal to the schools I went to. I just have one preacher, one wife, one barber, and one banker.

Do you have any idea about the source of that intense loyalty?

I think it was my mama first being loyal to me. I heard them in the next room when my mama was a teenager and had two little boys during the Depression. I heard them say, "The only hope is for you to give the boys up. I think we can place them at French Camp Academy. They can be up there and be orphans."

My mama would cry and say, "I'm going to keep my boys with me." I've seen her pick two rows of cotton (me and my brother trying to keep up picking one) and working and knocking off about eleven thirty to go to the house and try to scrape up something to eat—some hoecake or something out of an old meal barrel.

My mama is my number one hero.

Her being loyal to her babies, I think, was the first thing that started me to being loyal. I will stand hitched. I will stand with you. I think loyalty is the best policy. I was loyal to the navy. I was loyal to Mississippi Chemical. I'm loyal to my wife. I'm loyal to my children and to my grandchildren. And it just works. It's just common sense. It ought to be. It ought to work that way.

Are you still loyal to people when they do things you don't approve of?

You're loyal to them, too. If you don't approve of what they done, you still love them. And I've seen folks say, "If you do that ever again, I ain't going to have nothing else to do with you."

I did that with my own father one time. I looked him up. I hadn't seen him and didn't know where he was. I was a junior at Mississippi State and I went home. I was sittin' in the kitchen complaining about my daddy. There was a black woman ironing, and she said, "Boy, you'd better not criticize your daddy. The Bible says to honor your father and your mother. They're the ones that birthed you. It don't say honor your father and your mother if they don't drink whiskey. It just says honor your father and mother."

That got to just dwelling in my mind, and I caught the Rebel—a train in Artesia, Mississippi—and went to St. Louis and hunted my daddy. When I got ready to leave, I told him if he ever drank again I never would come back and see him. Then coming home on the train, I said, "Now, wasn't that silly? For me to claim to be a Christian, that was the most un-Christian thing I'd ever done in my life." I ought to have said, "I love you and I'm going to pray for you, and I hope your foot don't never slip again."

I remember Mr. Leroy Percy, who was the chairman of the board of Mississippi Chemical, telling a story about his uncle, William Alexander Percy, the one that wrote the books. William Alexander Percy called Leroy and his brother in as young men and give each one of them a hundred thousand dollars apiece. He said, "I want you to take this and make your fortune. I want to give it to you early so if you make a mistake and lose all of it, I can help you again." Mr. Leroy was the one who told me that. Isn't it beautiful?

And a lot of folks say, "You throw that away and you'll never get another dime from me." Not me, I'm just going to be loyal.

Years ago I called on Mr. Gaddis at Gaddis Farms in Utica. I set up his shipment of ammonium nitrate fertilizer from Mississippi Chemical. I had never met him before. I hadn't been with Mississippi Chemical for very long, and man, I was "big-dogging" it. I went back and turned in an order to ship a thousand tons.

When I got through writing up the order, I said, "Mr. Gaddis, you need some more ammonium nitrate?"

He said, "Yes, about five hundred tons."

I said, "Well, you don't have enough stock in the company to allow you to receive that additional tonnage, but there's a firm up in Missouri that's selling some of their stock, and I can get you some for so much a share."

He said, "Fine. I want that much stock. Draw a draft on me and just put it on the stock and ship all my fertilizer, whatever the discount is."

Well, I went back to Mississippi Chemical. I was so happy. I was drinking coffee and Mr. Cooper come walking in. I said, "I just sold all that stock that we have from the Missouri firm."

"Oh, you did?" he asked.

"Yes." And I told him how much a share it was.

Mr. Cooper said, "Jerry, I have friend up in the Delta; he sold his farm and he's moving to Florida. He needs to sell his stock, and we have enough buyers to buy the stock that you sold. Do you care if I call Mr. Gaddis and tell him that I can get this stock for him at fifty cents per share cheaper? The man would be pleased and it would help us to get a man's name off a stock certificate who don't own farm land."

I said, "No, sir. That would be fine."

So, he called Mr. Gaddis. Mr. Gaddis said, "Owen, that was such a fine young man, so mannerly. I shook his hand and made a deal with him."

Mr. Cooper said, "But Mr. Gaddis, you don't understand. He don't make a commission on the stock. He's sitting right here; he knows about it, and you haven't in any way told him anything that you won't live up to."

But Mr. Gaddis said, "Owen, I shook his hand and gave him my word. You leave that deal alone."

It's people like those who instilled in me loyalty and staying hitched. If people can't depend on you, then you ain't nothing. By the way, Mr. Gaddis owned eighty-four thousand acres of land. Wealthy, wealthy man, but he didn't get his wealth by shaking hands with people and telling them he'd do something and then not do it. He was true to his word. Now, that's loyalty.

You have mentioned Mr. Owen Cooper as an important influence in your life. Can you tell me more about him and his influence on you?

If the Lord gave me the ingredients and told me to make a man, I'd make him exactly like Owen Cooper. I knew him through his pocketbook, I knew him through his family, and I knew him through his business dealings. I've been under fire with him in business. I've been with him in good times. And I've seen him react every time exactly like you're supposed to if you claim to be a maximum, Bible-believing Southern Baptist Christian. And he never varied in dealing decently and in order with everybody. He was a remarkable, unbelievable person. And brilliant.

I remember one time me and my friend Charles Jackson from Yazoo City were trying to help a man get some cows back that broke out on the road. Charles said, "I wish Owen was here." I said,

"Why?" And he said, "Well, he'd be over yonder in that shade, and in about fifteen minutes he'd figure out a way that them cows would run and jump through that hole in the fence."

I've often said if I was on Death Row and had an hour to live before they threw that switch to electrocute me and they said, "Jerry, you've got just one more chance. You can name one person to start working on getting your sentence canceled." I'd say to notify Mr. Owen Cooper and let him work on it. And then I would have perfect peace. There wouldn't be no problem about me dying.

I miss him. [Cooper died in 1986.] Governor Ray Mabus called me the other day and requested that I do something, and as soon as I hung up the phone I wanted to call Mr. Cooper. I wanted his counsel. I miss him.

But I feel his arms around me every day. When I'm making decisions about my family and about my show business career, I remember the things he taught me. It's just like his arms are around me now. He still hovers over me like a mama hen, and I'm a biddy getting up under his wings.

What about you would have pleased your grandfather the most?

My granddaddy would be proud that I have a happy home and that I live where my roots are, that I still get excited when a neighbor brings me a mess of peas, and that I still love to go down and look at the baptizing hole where it all started. He would like knowing that I haven't left my own kind. He would be real pleased that I would name my daughter after his wife, Katy Burns, and that my son was so indoctrinated in his great-granddaddy and how much I respected him, that he named his little boy after him, Wesley Burns Clower.

Why do you think you did not succumb to the evils of show business—drinking, drugs, womanizing?

Because my career started late in life. I think I would have whipped it if I had a-started when I was twenty, but I might not have. I'm thankful every day that the Lord let me wait until I had some sense. I backed into show business when I was about forty-three years old. If I had been twenty-three, I might have been famous and sold a bunch of records but lost everything that's near and dear to me—my family and my friends. So the fact that I was stable and had both feet on the ground and was madly in love with Homerline and nobody could turn my head but her was very important. I'll never know, of course. I believe I would have been true to my faith if I had made a hit record at age twenty-one, but I might not have. The temptation was bad enough after I was forty-three. Somebody asked me one time what was the greatest temptation of any Christian, and I said, "Prosperity." Some folks don't sin because they can't afford to sin.

You use the term "bulldog, hang-on foreverishness" to describe what people need to be successful. The term certainly describes your nature. Where did it come from?

My mama. Because she hung on, or she couldn't have kept her babies.

When a bulldog gets a-hold of you, he won't turn loose. You've got to kill him before he'll turn loose. Only problem is sometimes he grabs what he's not supposed to. But the "bulldog, hang-on foreverishness" that I'm talking about is done decently and you ain't got a-hold of something you ain't supposed to bite. You're doing it right. Foreverishness: you've just *got* to do it.

If somebody wanted his child to have bulldog, hang-on foreverishness, how would he teach it?

In modern terms: teach children not to give up. A quitter never wins. Keep after it. Don't get discouraged and give up. "The sun don't shine on the same dog's behind all the time," to quote the late great Dudy Noble of Mississippi State University. So, go where the sun is shining. Fight! And grab a-hold. Hang on like a bulldog and don't give up, forever. Succeed!

Why do you still work so hard?

I like it. As long as the people want to buy a ticket, I'll keep performing. If I didn't, I'd just get fat and lazy and sit at home. I think I'm making a contribution.

My main motivation come from my mama. And, as I have said, I didn't ever want to be poor again or have any of my children poor. So I live real high. Folks say you can do too much for your children. Well, I'd rather be guilty of doing too much than hiding behind that excuse and not doing nothing.

But you have made all the money you could ever want and you are still on the road 200 days a year? Why?

There's more to it than money. Laughter is good for what ails you. It'll get people well. Hospitals use it. One of the wisest men that ever lived, King Solomon, said, "A merry heart doeth good like a medicine." That's in the book of Proverbs.

What about the joy of performing? The adrenalin? What makes the adrenalin flow?

I run out there on stage and if I can snatch 'em and get them motivated and get them with me, the adrenalin gets to flowing. I want to get them under that tree where me and Marcel's hollering, "Knock him out, John," or get them in that old car that me and Marcel trick the guy into pushing to see if it'll crank and there ain't even no motor in it. Or to see if they go with me on them fishing trips and on them coon hunts.

And sometimes the adrenalin gets to flowing when it's hot, and the audience is sitting on metal benches. (They ought to have had the blooming show at night.) And they're wanting a drink of water. And it motivates me that I've got to work hard to get them with me. They're hot and they're thinking about leaving. And I get fired up to hold them.

What do you get out of it when the adrenalin starts to flow?

When the show is over and I walk back toward my room, I have perfect peace and I have a feeling of elation that I done what I come to do. Ain't no feeling like that! Ain't no feeling like that of walking away from where you've performed knowing you've pleased the audience, you've pleased the man that hired you, and you've pleased the critic.

What about the applause? How does that affect you?

It's just like being hungry and you set down to a good bowl of peas and cornbread. The applause. It satisfies you. It pleases you. And I miss it when I'm not performing. I take off about three weeks at Christmas. I remember one day, I walked into the den. I said, "Homerline, all y'all are in here. I'm going to go back out and make an entrance. I want y'all to jump up and applaud. It's going to be the first part of January before people applaud me and I need this fix."

Homerline said, "Phftt!"

I know you have given a good deal of money to numerous charities and the church. You have established scholarships and things. Beside your family, do you have any certain place that you are going to leave your money?

I got scholarships at Mississippi State and Ole Miss and one at Holmes Community College and one at Southwest Mississippi Community College, and one at The Citadel. I have done this because I am blessed by doing it.

I've raised all of my children to be givers. I've raised all my children that they will never get unless they give. God won't bless them if they don't give. I'm going to leave all my money to my next of kin.

I have been a "storehouse tither": ten percent of every dime I make—the first ten percent—goes to the local church. The church is involved in the cooperative program in the missions and other programs that help people. I pray that my children will continue to be storehouse tithers and they will give and get involved in things like the Perch Jerking Tournament—the fishing rodeo to benefit the Mississippi Children's Hospital—and do things over and above the tithe with the money.

But as I sit here, according to my will, if I die today, every dime I've got goes to my wife, Homerline. Then, if she dies, everything goes to my younguns, and that gets back to that loyalty part. They're mine. I birthed them. So, I'll leave what I got to them.

Do you have any regrets about life?

No, because I give thanks for all things. I literally believe that. It's hard sometimes, but I believe that God ain't ever made a mistake, and he ain't going to make a mistake with me. So, whatever I do in my life today, I just say, "Thank you," and keep going. So, I don't have any regrets.

Oh, I would love to have played high school football and been trained in a sports program so when I got to the Southeastern Conference, I could have played up to my potential. I'd have been a big hoss and maybe made all-American or something.

But I get to thinking, hey, I give thanks for all things, and if I give thanks for all things, I can't have no regrets. So, no, I don't have any regrets.

Well, in show business, I do have one regret: I have never had my picture on a box of corn flakes! Before I get out of show business, I want my picture on a box of corn flakes. I would just love that!

Are you afraid of dying?

No, I'm not afraid of dying. I look forward to it. Heaven's my home. I ain't homesick and I hope He will let me stay here a good while longer and be able to fellowship with God's people and do what I'm doing and love my wife and my grandchildren and my children. But whenever the time comes, I look forward to it. It doesn't bother me a bit in the world.

How do you want to be remembered?

"He left the world better than he found it; he did it God's way."

There is a world-famous song that sold millions of records, "I did it my way." No. I think I did it my way to show business, but it's bigger than that. I did it God's way and I literally believed when I did it unto the least of these, I was doing it for the Lord. That was my motivation.

"He did it God's way." That's the way I'd like to be remembered.

This interview was conducted by JoAnne Prichard of the University Press of Mississippi.

GROWING UP COUNTRY

· · · · · W hen I was growing

up, there was five social functions that we

participated in: peanut boilings, candy pullings,

log rollings, rat killings, and coon hunts.

The Go-Gitter

I growed up with an ole boy I love very much. I won't tell you his real name, but we called him Hog. There was another ole boy in the community, he didn't make any bones about it, you ask him "What do you do?" he would say, "I'm a go-gitter. My wife works at the McComb Manufacturing Company, and every evening at 4:30 I go gitter." That's right. He is a go-gitter. He's been one all his life.

Well, we got another man in the community where I growed up, nosiest fellow in the world. I mean, he'd get up before daylight if he thought he could find out what chicken was going to get off the roost first. One day he was coming along and he saw the vehicles of old Hog and that "Go-Gitter" at the beer joint, so he stopped. He just decided he would discuss these men's occupations with them.

He sat down on the stool, and he looked at the "Go-Gitter" and said, "Sir, really now, what do you do?"

He said, "I don't do nothing. I am a go-gitter. Every evening at 4:30 I go get my wife. Every morning I take her to work. I'm a go-gitter. I don't do nothing."

Sitting over there by him was old Hog; had his elbows up on the counter. He said, "Hog, what do you do?"

He said, "I help him."

Peanut Boiling Was Required

When I was growing up, there was five social functions that we participated in: peanut boilings, candy pullings, log rollings, rat killings, and coon hunts. Peanut boilings. It was mandatory if you had a youngun in high school that was in the twelfth grade; if you wanted to be socially acceptable, you had to have a peanut boiling. Well, anybody that had a senior in high school when I was growing up would always plant a few extra rows of peanuts in the garden to have enough peanuts to boil.

When I come to Ocilla, Georgia, selling fertilizer, I called on a peanut farmer. I said, "Sir, what do you grow?" He said, "Peanuts."

I said, "How many rows you got?"

He said, "Six hundred fifty acres."

I said, "*Haaaaa!* You must have a lot of younguns in high school."

Rat Killin'

It was Monday morning and my mama told me to get on the school bus and tell all of my friends on there that we's gonna have a rat killin' Saturday. I got on the school bus, and I said, "We're gonna have a rat killin' Saturday."

Them folks come from all over the county with their dogs and sticks to help us kill them rats. We had worked our way to the far corner, and there was just a whole bunch of them rats flushed out of that corn crib at the same time. There was so many of them they broke through the ranks and run and got under a big concrete slab. We couldn't get them out from under there. We dug, drawed up water, and poured it down them holes trying to drown 'em.

Directly Uncle Versie Ledbetter, who was the head rat killer in our community, said, "Boys, I tell you what we got to do. If we can get that A-model car over there cranked, and back it up to that concrete slab, we can put that inner tube around the exhaust pipe and run the other end of that inner tube down under that concrete slab. If we get that old car cranked and go to racing that motor, I am told it manufactures something up in that engine that when you gush it down through that exhaust pipe, it will make the rats come out from under there." We got it cranked and revved that motor up. Now, folks, y'all ain't never had no fun unless y'all have stood with a stick waiting for them carbon monoxided, sick rats to come out of the front of that slab. Now that is some fun.

One day while we were having a rat killin', me and my brother, Sonny, was up in the corn crib, a-moving the corn and killin' them rats as we got to 'em. Directly my brother, Sonny, caught a bigun in the throat. It was the hugest rat I have ever seen in all my life. His tail hung way down. It was such a fine rat that my brother, Sonny, wanted to show it to Mama. He jumped out of the corn crib and commenced to running toward the house, hollering, "Mama, Mama, looka here what a rat!"

Now my brother, Sonny, didn't know that Reverend Brock, the Baptist preacher, was in the house visiting with Mama. But Sonny run on in the back door and run in the living room. Mama was sitting over in one corner and the preacher in the other. Now Sonny ain't seen the preacher yet. He rushed on into the living room and said, "Mama, looka here. What a rat! I done whipped him over the head with a ear of corn. I done jobbed him with a hayfork. I done stripped all the hide off of his tail. I done whopped him up and down on the floor of that corn crib. I done stomped him three or four times."

Then Sonny saw the preacher. And he hugged that rat up in his fist, and he commenced to stroking it and crying, "Oh, and then the Lord called the pore thing home!"

Rats in the Corn Crib

I was out there at Hollywood doing one of them talk shows, sitting on the couch, and had my feet propped up on the coffee table, watching my turn when I was supposed to go out on television. In walked a lady, and just as she walked in, she grabbed her Adam's apple and screamed "Ahhh, ahhh, ahhh!" Likened to have scared me to death.

I said, "Lady, what's the matter?"

She said, "Oh, look at your boots! Your boots are lizard boots, and some little creature had to be put to death. Some little creature had to be killed to give you your pair of lizard boots."

I said, "No, ma'am, a Greyhound bus run over this lizard. After the Greyhound bus run over this lizard, I run out there in the middle of the highway and fought the buzzards off of it. Then I made me a pair of boots."

She said, "Well, I've heard some of your records and you were talking about brutally killing a little rat."

I said, "Lady, you ain't serious—I mean, you ain't agin killing them rats."

She said, "You don't have to be so brutal."

I said, "Lady, I want to tell you something. This is a true story. Now you listen to me. I know you're a high society, city woman, but it's very obvious you're educated beyond your intelligence. Lady, let me explain something to you. Me and my brother, Sonny, used to work out in the fields. A rain would come and while we couldn't work in the field, Papa would send us to the corn crib and tell us to shuck and shell corn, getting ready to go to mill Saturday to get some corn meal ground for corn bread. It was bad enough with that old weevil dust getting up in my nose. (Achoo! We'd be sneezing.) But when we'd reach to get an ear of corn and our fingers would touch some wet shucks, we'd look and there'd be a stinking rat's nest messing up that corn crib.

Me and my brother, Sonny, would scoop up that stinking rat's nest, and we'd get them little old slick baby rats out of that nest. We had a big bird dog named Andy, and he was standing on the ground out there, flatfooted. We'd throw them little old slick baby rats out door, and old Andy would run and catch them whole in his mouth and swallow 'em."

That lady said, "Hahhh!" and broke and run from the dressing room and left me alone.

Cutworm Smith

When I was growing up, we played basketball on a dirt court. We took a crowbar and let two ride it and one pull it to line off the court. If you bounced the ball on that line, not only did it go out of bounds, but it ricocheted out. You never did have no squabbles.

Much has been said in recent years in the Southeastern Conference about the wrong man going to the free throw line and shooting the free pitch. Now, if that had happened at East Fork Consolidated High School when I was a youngun growing up, and the wrong fellow had a-went to the free throw line, not only would the five players on the team have stopped him, but Cutworm Smith would have jumped out of the stands and cut him with a pocket knife. We wouldn't put up with that.

A Double Fireplace

Me and my brother, Sonny, and my mama lived in a house one time what had a double fireplace. What that means is this: you sit in one room in front of the fireplace, and right directly across the back side of that fire is another fireplace what's hooked to the same chimney.

I was as scared of the dark as any youngun who ever lived, I'll guarantee you. My brother, Sonny, would always make me sit in front of this fireplace until I'd get so sleepy that I'd fall flat in the floor or either have to walk around in the dark by myself and go to bed.

One night he "sweated" me until I went on in there. I felt my way around through the kitchen and through the side room, and then back into the bedroom. When I got back into the bedroom on the other side of the fireplace, I saw Mama had moved the furniture.

Every night after I got in the bed, and got it warm, Sonny would take him a big running start—here he'd come—and he'd leave the floor and jump up on my back in the middle of that bed. That night, just as I walked in the room, I see the bed is right there by the door. It has been moved from across the room. Over yonder where the bed used to be is the chifforobe. I was laying there thinking, Do you reckon Sonny knows that Mama has moved this bed?

Directly I heard him coming. Bookity, bookity, booka. Here he come! I felt the air from him when he run by the door, from right there where I was laying. His feet left the floor, and it sounded like for several seconds he was up in the air. He come down flat of his stomach, and across that old wooden floor, and his head hit the wall on the far side of that room, right up under the chifforobe. Whoomm! And jarred the whole house.

Here come Mama with the lamp, holding it up over her head. "What in the world's happened to you younguns?" And I'm laying there in the bed giggling. "Hee, hee, hee!"

Sonny was squalling. We got him up out of the middle of the floor and lit the other lamp, and we picked splinters out of him and daubed mercurochrome on him till daylight. It took that long to get enough of mercurochrome on him where all them splinters had stuck into him.

Stealing Teacakes

One time when I was out in Hollywood, they put me in this big limousine and they drove me back to the airport. On the way I passed a bunch of folks doing some picketing. I told the limousine driver, "Slow down. What's this bunch of folks up to here?" I saw a big sign that said, "Death is cruel and unusual punishment. We are against it."

I said, "Stop, I want to talk to one of them fellows."

So he stopped that limousine and I spooled the window down and said, "What y'all doing?"

He said, "We don't want nobody killed for messing up." One of them big fancy ones—looked like he had one of them big sociology degrees—what had been eating onions, got right up in my face. "You're some kind of celebrity. I'm sure you're on our side. It has been proven that the penalty for crime does not deter crime."

I said, "Now wait a minute. You're over my head. Are you telling me the punishment for crime won't keep crime from happening? Is that what you're saying?"

He said, "That's exactly what I said."

I said, "Well, it's very obvious ain't none of y'all ever stole no teacakes from my mama and got caught." I said, "Fellow, I come in on the school bus one evening, changed into my other pair of over-alls, and went by the safe and stole two of them big pretty yellow teacakes. (Ahhh, you can eat that dough raw too—it's plumb yellow and good.) Mama done sprinkled that sugar on 'em and baked 'em. I was walking toward the cotton fields, and Mama said, 'Jer-ry.'

" 'Ma'am?'

" 'Did you steal any of them teacakes?'

" 'No, ma'am.'

"Well, about a hour later my mama caught me sitting on my cotton sack eating them teacakes. And when my mama got through with me, I never ever have ever stole another teacake.

"And I don't eat a cookie now of no kind that I don't call Mama and see if it's all right."

Steel Marbles

When I was a youngun growing up, the mainmost sport was mar-bles. (Whatever happened to playing marbles?) We'd draw a great big circle in the dirt and put the marbles in the center of the circle, and we'd get down on one knee and we would come to taw (the shooting line) and we'd shoot that good aggie—the taw, we called it—at the marbles. How many of them you knocked out was yours, and you could keep 'em if your mama didn't find it out.

I remember one time my brother, Sonny, he played hooky from school. Helped 'em build a highway one year. He'd help 'em work on them old bulldozers. One day they was working on that bulldozer and they done found some of them steel aggie ballbearings, and we never had seen none of them. He decided he'd come to school with five of them.

He gave me three of them. Then they piled all them marbles into that circle, and I got down there with that steel aggie. Oh man, I done busted up the game! We had a fellow named Ben DeLaughter. He was meaner in school than Marcel Ledbetter was. He was forevermore vicious, Ben DeLaughter. I was scared of him as I was a bear. Ben said, "I want you to give me one of them steel marbles."

I said, "I can't do it, man." He commenced whipping on me, and the bell rung, and we run in the school house. He was sittin' in that little old desk—been in the eighth grade eight times—and he would whisper, "I'm gonna beat you to death if you don't give me one of them big steel marbles."

I didn't know how in the world I was going to get away from Ben. But what I did was ease out of my desk and went back to the back of the room in the study hall like I was cold. I took two of them big steel aggies and put them up on top of the stove. I got them forevermore red scalding hot. I had me a brand new pair of them Red Rider gloves I had got for Christmas—had that fringe on the side right there, and Red Rider's picture up on the top. And when them steel aggies got hot—I mean forevermore hot—I went back there with my Red Rider gloves on, and I picked them up right quick and went and put them down in that little trench at the top of my desk what your pencil went in—right there by the hole where your ink bottle was supposed to go, but we never did have no ink.

Then when I laid them two hot aggies up there, I went to the pencil sharpener like I was going to sharpen my pencil. Miss Minnie Lee Stone, the teacher, she had us studying, and she was just sitting up there at her desk. Big Ben seen them aggies on my desk. He come easing up there, you know, like he wasn't up to nothing so the teacher wouldn't get on him. He had on a right new pair of overalls, and he just kind of squatted down and that back pocket was open right there. And he took his pencil and just raked them aggies in his back pocket, just like nothing had happened. He eased back to his desk and sat down right quick.

Ahh!! Aha!! Ohoo! Ben started jumping up and down in that desk and he hung in it—he was overgrown anyhow. Miss Minnie Lee Stone, the teacher, run up there with a big paddle and commenced to beating him.

"Ben, what you screaming about? Boy, you got ants in your pants?"

"No ma'am, hot steel balls!"

Justice for All

I remember during hard times, years ago, during the Depression, folks tried to be fair one with the other. I recall a man in the community who just didn't have anything. He had a rather large family and he stole a pair of mules from a man over on the other side of the county who had more than he did. He brought them mules in there late one night. Then he took a curry comb and he took some clippers and clipped them and brushed them down good, and then he changed their manes with them clippers. He made a crop with that pair of mules. Fed his family, too.

A constable doing routine police work caught him, arrested him, and he was tried at Liberty, Mississippi, the county seat of my home county. The jury listened to the case. The jury came back into the courtroom and they said, "We find this man innocent, and he can give the mules back to the man."

The judge throwed a fit. He said, "There ain't gonna be this kind of justice in my court, I won't put up with this. This is about the most stupid thing I've ever heard of in my life. You jurors get back in there and you bring out a verdict commensurate with the type of testimony you heard here this morning. This man stole these mules. We got to have justice. Whoever heard of such a man being innocent, and he could give the mules back?"

So the jury went back in there, deliberated about fifteen minutes, and come back out. The foreman of the jury got up.

"Have you reached a verdict?"

"We have. We find the man innocent, and he can keep the mules."

Mr. Duvall Scott's Chicken

Right after the Depression when ice trucks first started running out into the county, if you had a few pennies, you could buy you a hunk of ice. Well, Mr. Duvall Scott made him a wooden icebox and started selling frying-size chickens in his store. (Why, I have carried a frying-size chicken to Mr. Duvall Scott and I have swapped that chicken for a jar of antipain oil or a jar of vanilla extract.) Then Mr. Duvall Scott would pick the chicken, dress it, and put it in the icebox with the little chipped-up ice down in there.

One day I was sitting in the store when a lady walked in and said, "I'd like to buy a chicken."

He didn't have but one in that whole icebox deal he had made. So, he reached down in there and switched it around in that water and the few little blocks of ice. Then he brought it out, slung the water off of it, laid it on the scales, and said, "It weighs two and a half pounds."

She said, "I was wanting one just a little bit bigger." So he took that one chicken and rammed it back down in there, and started stirring that ice again, stirring it good. He brought it out and put it up there again. "Three pounds."

She said, "That's fine, but I'll take both of 'em."

Chittlins

When I was a little boy, I used to go quail hunting. They wouldn't let me shoot no gun, but the adults in the community would let me pick up the birds when they shot 'em.

Well, we was hunting and we was cold, and that dinner bell rung. And we walked up there, and there was an old man and an old woman, and as luck would have it they was killing hogs.

"Y'all come on in before the fire and warm while she's fixin' dinner."

Well, we went in the house—me and my two adult friends—and the old man was sitting in the chair warming before the fire, and the old woman was setting the table right behind us.

Now, this old man had a boy off in the war. His son had sent him a pair of old leather britches, and he'd wore them so much they done cracked and busted open down here in the stride. The straps of them britches had just split all back here, but he was wearing them—still had 'em on. He was sitting up there in that cane-bottom chair and part of his flab was sticking through a crack in that cane-bottom chair. Part of his flab, his body, had done wadded up and scroonched down through that crack in them britches. He kinda moved around in that chair, and he done kind of wadded it down through the crack in that cane-bottom chair.

Well, the old lady was walking with the plates and she saw it. She said, "Oh, my goodness! That bloomin' cat's brought a chittlin in this house. I'll be embarrassed to tears if these visitors in my home see that chittlin hanging under that chair."

The old lady got around there and took the tongs that you punch up the fire with, walked around and started punching them logs and turning them with the tongs—fixing the fire for her visitors where we could warm good. Then she just put the tongs down by her, walked over around behind us, all of us still looking straight ahead at the fire.

Then that dear old lady got down on one knee and took them tongs; she was going to ease that chittlin out from under that chair and go throw it out in the yard. Bless her soul! She got down there and she opened up them tongs, and eased 'em under there to fit 'em onto that chittlin, and was going to ease down on 'em to pull it out from under that chair.

Wowee! With few exceptions, I ain't never seen a room tore up that bad in my life!

Go Vote

I listened to a talk show on the radio one day when I was driving to Tuscaloosa, Alabama. This fellow was on there and he was cussing politicians. He was giving them up the country: how low down they was, they all ought to be voted out of office.

The talk show host on the radio said, "But, sir, what is the name of your state senator and your state representative?"

"What? Ahh. . ."

"You don't know who they are?"

"Well, now, I'm not into that too much, but I . . ."

Now, I got sick. It's one thing not to know who they are, but don't let nobody know you don't know. Just stay ignorant and don't let nobody know you're ignorant.

I'm gonna write that talk show host a letter. I think that's a good question. Every time somebody calls and goes to griping, just say, "Did you vote? Are you a qualified elector?" I can't fathom people not exercising their right of franchise and voting.

When I was a little bitty boy, my grandpaw got up before daylight one morning and left the house. He was gone all day, and he come back in after I went to bed. This went on for three days, and the fourth morning I got up and he was there.

I said, "Big Daddy, where have you been?"

He said, "I been doing public work—working for the county."

"Why?"

He said, "We have a poll tax we have to pay before we can vote, and I didn't have two dollars to pay it. So the county agreed to let me work three days and they would pay me two dollars."

And his face lit up and he said, "Hallejuh! I done earned two dollars. I can vote! Thank God. Boy, your granddaddy is going to be able to vote."

My grandpaw—building bridges, working with his hands, daylight to dark, because he didn't want to miss out on having the privilege of voting. And I ain't ever going to let that old man down. I fix my schedule to where I can go vote. I vote against some of 'em, some of 'em I vote for, but I vote. I urge you to.

Why Can't Johnny Read?

Every now and then I get aggravated. Here lately I been reading in the paper, hearing on the radio, and watching on the TV, and everybody is saying, "Why can't Johnny read?" I got to thinking about this.

The other day I read about a bunch of Ph.D's and some folks what met for about three days at a seminar. At the end of the seminar they commenced to telling people why Johnny can't read. I got sick at some of the reasons they gave. One of them learned fellows said the reason Johnny can't read no better than he can is due to the energy crisis. Johnny didn't get to go to school enough.

The main reason Johnny can't read is: Johnny don't give a care whether he can read or not. Now, I ain't talking about them folks that's handicapped or got bad eyes. I'm talking about folks that are able-bodied, but yet the society we live in today tells them how underprivileged they are and how awful it is they weren't born into affluency. This is the United States of America: if you want to do it and you got that bulldog, hang-on foreverishness, you can be a winner!

Another reason Johnny can't read is that Johnny's mama and daddy don't give a care whether he can read or not. They ain't interested in him. When they find out he can't read, then they go to blaming the teacher of the school. I know some of them people. I've talked to them about it. I say, "Listen here. What's your little boy's teacher's name?"

They'd say, "We don't know. Never have met her."

Yeah, that makes a lot of sense, don't it? They find out he can't read, then they get to looking for a patsy. They want to blame it on somebody else, when they ought to be more concerned about their own child. Parents and guardians ought to be more concerned about whether their children can read.

But don't tell me it's the energy crisis.

Let me tell you about the energy crisis we had at East Fork Consolidated High School when I went to school—we didn't have no energy crisis, 'cause we didn't have no energy of no kind. We didn't have no running water, we didn't have no natural gas, we didn't have no electricity. We had a big wood heater; if you got cold, you put some wood in there and built a fire. When you wanted to go to the bathroom, you raised your hand and said, "Teacher, may I go under the hill?"

Those of us in that underprivileged school that wanted to learn how to read, learned how. We learned how to read.

Talk about not going to school enough. We started in September and didn't go but half a day, because we got out early to pick cotton. Then when spring would come along after Christmas, we would get out half a day to go home and plow and plant crops. We didn't have but eight months school all told, and we didn't go but half of the time then. But those of us who wanted to learn how to read had mamas and daddys that told us we wasn't underprivileged—we had the right to learn how to read if we wanted to. I studied by coal oil lamp. If some of the people of today had a known the situation I was in, they'd a told me how bad off I was, and I'd a probably growed up not being able to read. But nobody told me!

The other day I got to thinking about them eight folks that finished East Fork Consolidated High School in the year 1944. Whatever happened to that underprivileged bunch that went to that school during that energy crisis?

The first one I can think of, he's a retired army colonel. The next one, he's a retired commander, served in the United States Navy. The next one became very wealthy from real estate. The next one, he's a top chemist for a petrochemical company. The next one, he's a top geologist for a big oil company. The other two—they were girls—married well. And the last one: those people who vote on such matters have said for twelve years that he is the number one country comic in all the world!

Judgment in the Sky

Down at East Fork Community of Amite County, Mississippi, I had the privilege of growing up with a gentleman by the name of Kirk Garner. Kirk Garner was a very religious fellow. He was in church every time them church doors opened.

One day he walked out on his front porch and an airplane had just finished doing some skywriting. Kirk didn't know that no airplane could do that. The airplane was gone, and the words what that plane wrote was kinda fading out. Kirk stood on the front porch and looked at it, then broke and run back in the house and told his wife, "Cally, it's Judgment. God done wrote it in the sky."

Cally said, "I don't hear no horns blowing and no bells ringing. I don't believe it's Judgment."

It aggravated Kirk to the extent he broke and run, jumped off the front porch, tripped and fell over a faucet he had drove into the ground to make folks think he had running water. (Actually, Kirk toted water a mile and a half from a branch back behind his house. He had a great big antenna stretched across the roof of his house, and Kirk didn't even know what a radio was.) He hit that road and he started running toward my daddy's house, and he was kicking up dust, brother. He was scared to death that Judgment was there.

Mr. Halley, a man down the road, saw him coming and knew something was bad wrong with Kirk running that fast, kicking up that much dust. He got out in the middle of the road and bear-hugged him when he come by. "Slow down, Kirk. What in the world is happening?"

He said, "Mr. Halley, it's Judgment."

"Why would you say that, Kirk?"

"I saw it wrote in the sky. God's done wrote it up there."

Mr. Halley said, "Kirk, that's Pepsi Cola."

"Sir?"

"That's Pepsi Cola, Kirk. An airplane wrote that up there. The airplane's been gone for several minutes, and you just saw that writing."

"Oh, Mr. Halley, you know that ain't no Pepsi Cola."

"Yes, it is. That plane wrote it and has done gone. You just calm down, it ain't Judgment."

The next morning Kirk came down to my daddy's house, and they were standing out in the back yard and Kirk was telling my daddy this story. Daddy asked him, "Kirk, what would you have done had it been Judgment?"

He said, "I was just gonna keep running till Judgment overtook me."

A FAMILY
NAMED LEDBETTER

. . . . . **T**hey were my closest

neighbors, and they was great people. As I think

back on my childhood days, there is nobody I

loved more than the whole family of Ledbetters.

The Burning Building

I growed up at Route 4, Liberty, Mississippi, with a family named Ledbetter. They were my closest neighbors, and they was great people. As I think back on my childhood days, there is nobody I loved more than the whole family of Ledbetters. Uncle Versie was the mainmost one: he was the papa of them all.

Our county seat town was a small town with a volunteer fire department. It was in the middle of the summer—big drought, no water. Everybody knew if a building caught on fire, it was gone, 'cause there wasn't no water. We just couldn't draw it up fast enough to put out no fire.

One Saturday evening this building caught on fire, and commenced to burning. The crowd gathered, their arms folded, squalling, watching the building burn 'cause there ain't no water.

About that time here come Uncle Versie Ledbetter and Aunt Pet, his wife, in their old truck. Had all the younguns with them—Ardell, Burnell, Raynell, W. L., Odell, Udell, Lanell, Marcel, Claude, Newgene, and Clovis. They was all hanging on that old truck.

Everybody heard them coming, the fenders rattling, bumpada bumpa bump—here they come. And the crowd parted 'cause they was coming pretty fast. They run right on up the sidewalk and right up in the middle of the fire—into the fire! And they jumped off and took off their overall jumpers, and went to flopping and stamping the fire. Aunt Pet had her bonnet, telling them, "Here, stamp over here; beat it out." And they stamped the fire out! They put it slap out.

The folks cheered, "The Ledbetters, they're heroes. They put out the fire." They passed the hat and took up a collection—thirty-one dollars—and give the money to Uncle Versie. They said, "Sir, we love you. Y'all are heroes. Tell us, what you gonna buy with the thirty-one dollars?"

He said, "The first thing I'm gonna do is get the brakes fixed on that truck!"

The Last Piece of Chicken

If you ask an adult old as I am, what growed up in the country, he'll tell you we were taught some manners when we were younguns. We had manners, I'll tell you now. Never, ever, would you be caught taking the last piece of chicken off the plate, or the last biscuit. Now, you'd sit there and want it some kind of bad, but you knowed better than to take it off the plate.

I finished supper one evening and went over to the Ledbetter house, and they was eating supper. They was all sitting around the table there: Marcel and Claude and Newgene and Aunt Pet Ledbetter. Well, they was all sitting around the table, and there was one piece of chicken left right in the middle of the platter. All of them was a-sitting there looking at it.

A wind come up and blowed the lamp out, and you could hear Uncle Versie scream just like lightning had struck him.

Aunt Pet jumped up and finally got the lamp lit, and there was five forks sticking in the back of Uncle Versie's hand.

The Grassers

Where I come from we have muscadines. Sometimes we refer to them as bullices or scuppernongs. Them Ledbetters would get them water buckets and they'd take to the swamp when them muscadines was ripe, and they'd pick them water buckets full of them muscadines. They loved them muscadines. They'd make jelly out of 'em, and take the pulp left from squeezing the juice out of them hulls, and they'd dump 'em in a barrel in the smokehouse, and let it ferment. They'd put some good muscadines in there too, and stomp on 'em, sqush 'em up.

Now, the Ledbetter family had seventeen geese. They were known as "grassers." See, if you had a cotton crop, a goose would eat the grass out of that crop. Uncle Versie had seventeen geese, and they'd go down through that cotton patch and eat all of that grass out of there.

Well, one Sunday the Ledbetters was at church, and them geese got to smelling the aroma of them muscadines in that barrel. That aroma flung a craving on them geese. They got to pecking at the door of that smokehouse, got a hole in there, and they all got up in that smokehouse. They pecked on the staves on that barrel. They finally got a hole in it, and out come that fermented muscadine juice right out on them geese. And they drunk a bait of it—every one of them.

When the Ledbetters come home from church there were seventeen geese laying on their backs, with their legs sticking straight up in the air.

Uncle Versie said, "Wonder what in the world killed these geese? We can't eat 'em, 'cause we don't know what killed 'em. At least we can pick all the feathers off of 'em and make us a featherbed mattress."

So them Ledbetters—Arnell, Burnell, Raynell, Lanell, W. L., Odell, Udell, Marcel, Claude, Newgene and Clovis, Aunt Pet and Uncle Versie—grabbed 'em a goose and here they went, a-picking them feathers. They got 'em all picked, throwed 'em in a wagon, took them down the hill to a creek, and throwed them seventeen geese all in the creek. They were floating on their backs, going down the creek.

This creek is fed by an underground, cold, cold spring. That water is cold and invigorating. All of them Ledbetters was back at the house, ramming them feathers in that bed ticking, and Udell hollered, "Oh, look coming yonder! Look coming yonder!"

Walking up in the yard was seventeen naked geese!

The New Chandelier

One time they called a deacons' meeting at the East Fork Church. Uncle Versie Ledbetter was up in years, and he didn't go to many of the deacons' meetings no more because he thought the young folks, them about fifty and sixty, could take care of the church business. But he got word they was fixing to spend some money, and he got Newgene, his grandson, to take him over to the church house in a mule and wagon for the deacons' meeting.

The deacons got in a big discussion about buying a chandelier for the church. A man said, "I move, sir, that we buy a chandelier for the church."

Another deacon said, "I second the motion."

The moderator said, "Is there any discussion?"

Uncle Versie Ledbetter said, "Sir, I would like to speak. I want all of you to know that if we gonna buy a chandelier, there ain't nobody in our church got enough education that, when we order it from Sears and Roebuck, they could spell it. Then if we ordered the chandelier, when it got here, there's nobody here in our church that knows how to play it. And what I'm concerned about is we don't need to spend this money on no chandelier as bad as we need lights in the church."

Johnson Grass

One time, Uncle Versie Ledbetter had seen a wreck out on the highway. Uncle Versie was a witness that the big old bus did run over the mule and wagon. He testified, standing before the jury, put his hand on the Bible and swore before God that the bus was doing seventy miles an hour when it run into the mule and wagon.

The smart aleck lawyer—yeah, a little old smart aleck lawyer—looked up at Mr. Versie Ledbetter. "Are you sure you could see that? How far can you see?"

Uncle Versie said, "I can see the moon. How far is that?"

The lawyer said, "You're willing to swear before God that the bus was doing seventy miles an hour, and you ain't even on the bus; you just walking alongside the highway?"

"That's right. I swear before God."

"Well, will you please face the jury and tell the jury why you would swear that you know the bus was going seventy miles an hour and you can't even see the speedometer?"

He said, "I knew the bus was going seventy miles an hour as to how the Johnson grass bowed down side the road when it passed."

Uncle Versie's Trial

Not long ago I done drove to Uncle Versie Ledbetter's house. Aunt Pet, his wife, was sittin' on the front porch, squalling. I said, "Aunt Pet, something must be bad wrong."

She said, "They got Versie down there at the courthouse!"

I said, "Uncle Versie Ledbetter ain't never done nothing to be tried in a courthouse in his life."

She said, "They got him down there, Jerry."

I took off down there, and it was dinner time. I walked across the lawn and there was the district attorney. I said, "What have y'all done to Uncle Versie?"

He said, "Jerry, he had a wreck. He said one thing at the wreck and something else later."

"What do you mean? Uncle Versie ain't never lied in his life."

He said, "Well, he's fixing to take the witness stand. Come on in the courtroom and watch him."

Uncle Versie took the witness stand and raised his hand. The little fancy lawyer got up and said, "Mr. Ledbetter, didn't you, sir, at the scene of the wreck, say there wasn't nothing wrong with you, and now you claim to have a broke leg and you want the insurance company to fix it?"

Uncle Versie said, "That's right."

The lawyer said, "Would you mind facing the jury and telling in your own words, please, why you lied then and you are changing your mind now?"

Uncle Versie said, "I wouldn't mind doing it a bit in the world." He went on: "I loaded up a hog and I was taking that hog to town to the sale barn to sell it. About halfway into town, one of them great big double-decker trucks, loaded down with cows, sideswiped me in a curve, turned over on me, knocked me down in the ravine, and them cows poured out on me bellowing and broke all to pieces. I thought I was a goner. I'm laying down there with a broke leg, and all them bellowing and bleeding cows.

"Up walked one of them big state troopers with them black boots on. He moved his coat around a big .357 magnum and pulled out that magnum and asked the truck driver, 'What's wrong with that there cow down there?'

"'That cow's got a broke leg.'

"Ah! He shot her right 'tween the eyes. That trooper asked that truck driver, 'What's wrong with that cow over yonder?'

"'Got a broke leg.'

"Boom! Shot her right 'tween the eyes. 'What's wrong with that cow over yonder squirming and bellowing?'

"'She's got a broke leg.'

"Boom. Shot her right through the head, killed her graveyard dead.

"That gun was smoking, that trooper had the barrel of that thing tilted a little bit, and he looked down there at me and said, 'Sir, what's wrong with you?'

"I said, 'Not a thing in the world.'"

Uncle Versie's Bond

I growed up with some folks that didn't have much education. They was supposed to be kind of dumb, but Uncle Versie Ledbetter was one of the smartest human beings I've ever known in my life. Uncle Versie has done wireworked it around where he's got a few oil leases, and he's done sold a few old cows, til he's done right well.

I remember a few years ago, I went home and everybody in town was laughing. Uncle Versie had been to town and he walked in the bank and walked up to a teller. He talked to her, and she pointed him to a big executive sittin' in the lobby of the bank. Uncle Versie went over and sat down with this big executive and said, "Sir, I want to borrow some money."

The bank executive said, "Oh, Mr. Ledbetter, what is your collateral?"

Uncle Versie said, "I got a $10,000 bond."

The man said, "All right, I'll loan you any amount of money you want to borrow up to $10,000 and we'll take the bond for collateral."

Uncle Versie said, "That's fine. I want to borrow a dollar for a year."

The banker said, "Well, we ain't gonna loan nobody just a dollar."

Uncle Versie said, "Well, you lied then, you said you would. You said you would loan me any amount of money up to $10,000."

He said, "I did tell you that. This is very unorthodox, and I won't go back on my word. Yes, sir. Sign here. Here's the dollar you are borrowing. Give me the bond and I'll put it in the safe for safekeeping."

Uncle Versie come back in at the end of the year. He said, "I'm ready to pay off that note." He gave the banker a dollar and fifteen cents interest. He got his old note and the bond and started out the bank.

The banker said, "Mr. Ledbetter, it would be of much interest to me if you would tell me why you just borrowed a dollar from this bank on your $10,000 bond?"

Uncle Versie said, "I came in here a year ago and I needed a place to keep this bond that was a safe place for a year. I talked to your teller and she said a lockbox would be twenty-four dollars a year. I borrowed a dollar from you, and you kept the bond for me in a safe place all this year for fifteen cents."

Peanuts

Aunt Pet Ledbetter eats fatback meat, sorghum molasses, and all the corn bread and collard greens she can hold. She's eighty-seven years old and going strong. Oh, she can work down young women. Only thing that put her in the hospital is her teeth. They had to pull all of Aunt Pet Ledbetter's teeth.

They put her in the Southwest Regional Hospital in southwest Mississippi. They put her to sleep and pulled all of her teeth at the same time—she only had sixteen of them left.

The next morning the preacher went by to see Aunt Pet. "I'm so glad you are doing well. Good to see you. The church is praying for you."

Sitting right there on the nightstand by the bed was a bowl of peanuts. The preacher reached over and got him one of them peanuts and commenced to eating it. He talked to Aunt Pet, and then he'd eat another one—you just can't stop at eating one. Directly he prayed and got up and said, "I've got to go. But, Mrs. Ledbetter, I'll be back to see you in the morning, and I'll bring you another bowl of peanuts."

"Good gracious alive! Don't bring me no peanuts, 'cause I can't bite 'em. I won't be able to eat no peanuts, sore as my gums are, until I get my new teeth. What I do is suck the chocolate off of 'em and put the peanuts back in that bowl."

Hitler on the Front Porch

Now, you got to be real country to understand what I'm about to tell you. Marcel Ledbetter didn't register for the draft, and the FBI come after him.

Uncle Versie said, "What y'all want with Marcel?"

They said, "He didn't register for the draft."

Uncle Versie said, "He ain't about to register for it."

"Well, there's a war going on and he's supposed to fight."

Uncle Versie said, "That don't make no difference. He ain't gonna fight cause y'all stupid. I hear one man started all this fight—named Hitler. And why y'all don't just kill him and stop it, I'll never know. If it was a bunch of folks after us, it'd be different. But Hitler, they tell me, can control it and y'all ought to go kill him."

They said, "Well, Mr. Ledbetter, they can't get to him."

He said, "Don't lie to me. They can stand at the end of his front porch about bedtime, he's got to come out there some time."

Runaway Truck

I want to salute the truckers of America. I tell my daughters when they get out on the highway and their car breaks down, flag down a trucker. Them good ole boys, they'll help you.

Ardell and Burnell Ledbetter took a test one time to be truckers. They took the driving part of it and done good. The man what was giving the test, working with the highway patrolman, said, "Y'all come to such and such a building on such and such a day, and you can take the written and oral part of this truck driving test."

Ardell and Burnell showed up. They give 'em the written test, and they passed it. Then the highway patrolman said, "Now, I'm gonna give the oral part of it. Ardell Ledbetter, you driving this truck, you top a hill, you see down at the bottom blue lights are flashing, the 'syringes' are blowing, bodies are laying side of the road. There ain't nothing for you to do but take to the ditch. What's the first thing you're gonna do when you pull off the shoulder and head toward the ditch? Tell me now, what's the first reaction you will have in your mind when you leave the road? Answer it."

Ardell said, "I'm gonna wake up Burnell."

"My goodness, man, you gonna wake up your brother, Burnell. Why?"

"Burnell ain't never seen no bad truck wreck before."

Sitting Up with the Dead

Where I come from, we still sit up with the dead. When I was a boy there was no exceptions to this, none whatsoever. Nowadays, we done got kind of fancy. The funeral home director may get up at ten o'clock and say, "The funeral home is closed, and we'll open back up in the morning at seven o'clock."

Well, we was having a funeral in southwest Mississippi the other day, and that funeral director got up and made that announcement, and Uncle Versie Ledbetter said, "Sir, you go right ahead and close your funeral home, but my friend and neighbor, Brother Zias, is dead, and I want you to know that we ain't gonna leave him here by himself. Now, you shut the front door and go on home, but I'm gonna make two of my boys stay here with him all night. Clovis and Newgene Ledbetter, they gonna be here with him. Now they won't get in your way. They'll just be sittin' in here by my dead friend, all night."

Everybody left, and in about thirty minutes Clovis could see a neon light on a beer joint over yonder across the road. Clovis said, "Newgene, I believe I'll step over yonder and get us something to drink."

Newgene said, "Un unh, I ain't staying here with him by myself. I'll run over there and get us something."

Clovis said, "Naw, I ain't about to stay here with him by myself neither. I understand there's four more down the hall."

They sat there about another hour, and they could see that neon light on over there. And they got to smacking their lips, and their mouths got dry as cotton. Directly they decided they'd go to the beer joint and get them something to drink, and just take the dead man with them.

So they got him up, and one got on one side and one on the other. They stood him up between them and they started walking to the beer joint. Every now and then they'd let the dead fellow's foot drag in the middle of the road where people would think he was stepping right along with them. They went on in the beer joint, and stood him up at the counter, put one of them four-legged stools right behind him, and wedged him in there. And there he was.

Clovis was over there on one side drinking and Newgene was over here on the other. The dead man was the best dressed man in the whole beer joint. About that time a fight broke out—a fist fight, busting chairs over one another's head. Somebody took their fist and hit Uncle Zias right side of the head and cut him a flip right out in the middle of the floor.

Here come the police, lining them up, handcuffing them, searching them. Clovis saw Uncle Zias in the middle of the floor, and he fell down there by him, and put his arm under his head, and commenced to screaming and crying. He pointed to a fellow and said, "You killed him! You killed him! I saw you when you hit him, you killed him! You killed him!"

The sheriff went over and handcuffed the fellow. The fellow said, "Sheriff, wait a minute, I did hit the fellow, but it was self-defense. He pulled a pocket knife on me."

Newgene Ledbetter

Newgene Ledbetter was the meanest youngun that's ever been in southwest Mississippi. He holds the record yet. Uncle Versie spent about half of his time whippin' Newgene. Now he was forevermore mean! Just into something all the time.

I remember one day Aunt Daisy DeLaughter went over there, walked from her house to take one of them there mission books to Mrs. Ledbetter. They was going to try to study some kind of book, and Aunt Daisy could read. Aunt Daisy walked up the front step and she heard something growling, and dust was coming up from under the door steps. There come Newgene out from under the steps on his all fours, growling and barking like a dog, and he bit Aunt Daisy on the leg—just bit a chunk out of her leg.

"Boy, get back! What in the world are you doing?"

He said, "I'm playing dog."

Uncle Versie run out there and he got a brush broom and commenced to whipping Newgene. "I told you about that dog game you play. You done bit Aunt Daisy."

They brought her in the house and set her down on the bench what set alongside the dining room table. Newgene come walking in.

Uncle Versie said, "You gonna tell her you're sorry for biting her."

Aunt Daisy said, "Oh, I just know you want to be a sweet little boy."

Newgene said, "Sweet? You want something sweet?" And he reached and grabbed the syrup pitcher, popped the top off, and turned that syrup pitcher bottom upwards on Aunt Daisy's head. And that syrup commenced to pouring down over her ears and running in her hair.

Uncle Versie carried him out in the back yard and commenced to beating him. You could have heard him all over that county. I run out there and said, "Please, Uncle Versie, don't beat Newgene no more. This is awful. Let him go to the swimming hole with me."

He said, "All right. But you water them chickens, Newgene, before you go."

Newgene run out there and raised up a chicken coop and caught four of the biggest, finest fryers you ever saw. He come back and jobbed them down in the water well, and let the bucket down on 'em, and said, "Y'all drink. Drink plenty of it."

Now folks, they drawed feathers, chicken bones, and every other kind of thing you can imagine out of that well. It took about six months to draw it out clean enough where they could drink water out of it.

Newgene was forevermore bad—bad awhile. I recall one time me and my brother, Sonny, was going to the grist mill—that's where you take corn to have it ground up for corn bread. We was driving by the Ledbetter house with our mules and wagon, when we heard the awfullest racket you ever heard in all your life. My brother, Sonny, stopped the mule and wagon. He said, "Jerry, listen. That sounds like some kind of animal in distress."

I said, "Man, let's get away from here. That's some kind of varmint."

Sonny said, "That's coming out from behind the Ledbetter house. Ain't no telling what Newgene's doing."

About that time, coming around the house from the back side, was a black and tan hound what was howling. He had his paws up over his eyes, barking, and he was as white as he could be. It was obvious soap suds was all over him. He was scratching and rolling over on the ground, and bellowing, and Sonny said, "Man, tie these mules, and let's go around there and see what in the world is going on."

We walked around to the porch, and there was Newgene Ledbetter. He had four hounds up in a washing machine. Uncle Versie had the only washing machine in Amite County. It had one of them gasoline engines, with one of them boards in there that splashed back and forth, back and forth. Newgene had four black and tan hounds over in there, and had his mama's batting board and a great big box of Octagon soap powder. Every time one would stick his head up, Newgene would shove it back down in there.

Sonny said, "Newgene, what are you doing?"

Newgene said, "I'm gonna wash these dogs if it takes the rest of the evening."

We finally got him to let them dogs out of that washing machine and come on and go to the grist mill with us.

The Fish and the Edsel

Newgene Ledbetter was a full-blood, registered, pedigreed liar. I went to a funeral the other day. Somebody said, "Jerry, old Newgene, he's turned over a new leaf. He don't lie every time he opens his mouth."

Newgene was there setting up at the funeral home, about two o'clock in the afternoon. Folks was up at the casket squalling, so I knew I could risk sitting down in there and he wouldn't come over there and tell me no lie.

Well, it wasn't long before he eased over there by me, said, "Jerry, I put this old Edsel car in the lake. I knew it would be a good cover for them old mossy backed bass fish to get in there. I left that Edsel in that lake about six months. I got my rod and reel, I went down there, and I parked my boat right up over that Edsel. I throwed that old plug out there, and about a fourteen-pound big-mouthed bass grabbed it. It run up in the back seat of that Edsel, and I was spooling him in. I'm turning that spool, and I'm tightening up that line, and I'm about ready to pull him out of the back seat of that Edsel, and Jerry, he rolled the window up on me!"

Newgene and the Lion

Some folks will take advantage of dogs. They'll be done messed up and done something, and they'll blame it on a dog. Newgene Ledbetter was like that.

Newgene was the meanest Ledbetter of them all. He used to even play dog—get down on his all fours and get up under the front porch. Somebody walked up in the front yard, he'd come out from under there, barking. One day he bit Aunt Daisy DeLaughter on the leg. Uncle Versie beat him. And lie—Newgene would climb a tree to tell you a lie when he could stand on the ground and tell the truth.

I was over there eating supper with them one night. I had been swapping work with the Ledbetters. Am I talking over your head? Swapping work, see, I growed up pore and we didn't have no money. A lot of times we had to get neighbors to come in and help us do work. It's hard to pull a crosscut saw by yourself. And I had been getting Newgene to come and help me saw stove wood. Now I was over there paying back a day's work by helping them dig a dug well.

Aunt Pet Ledbetter said, "Jerry, you want to stay and eat supper with us?" Did I ever! 'Cause she made them big old cathead biscuits, squshed them up with her hands, cooked them golden brown. You bite into one of them, it'd make a puppy pull a freight train.

There I'm sitting, with old Newgene, the lying Ledbetter, and all of the other Ledbetters—Arnell, Burnell, Raynell, W. L., Lanell, Odell, Udell, Marcel, Claude, Newgene and Clovis. We was eating supper, and Newgene jumped and hollered, "*Hahhh!* There's a lion in the yard! There's a lion in the yard. He's gonna eat us up!"

Uncle Versie looked out there and there was a dog in the front yard, a big old collie dog. It was hot summertime and somebody had sheared all the hair off that dog, and had left a ring of hair around his neck and a patch of hair right on the end of his tail. Uncle Versie wheeled around and slapped Newgene down, flat of his back, and stood straddle of him.

He said, "Boy, I done told you about lying. I done begged you to quit. You're a pretty good boy, but you just lie so much I can't depend on you. Newgene, I'm gonna turn it over to the Lord. I don't know nothing else to do but let God take it over. You get up out of that floor, go out yonder in the side room, and you get down on your knees and you beg God to forgive you of the sin of lying. Go now and do it."

Newgene come back in about fifteen minutes. Uncle Versie said, "Newgene, you feel better?"

"Yessir."

"You feel like you can overcome the temptation of lying?"

"Yessir."

"You feel better inasmuch as you told the Lord to help you?"

"Yessir."

Newgene said, "In fact, Papa, while I was out there talking to the Lord, the Lord talked directly back to me."

Uncle Versie said, "Newgene, son, don't lie about God!"

Newgene said, "I ain't lying, no sir. The Lord talked just as plain to me while I was out there as I can hear your voice talking to me right now."

Uncle Versie said, "You mind sharing with us what the Lord told you?"

Newgene said, "No, I don't mind telling you. The Lord told me the first time he saw that dog, he thought it was a lion, too."

Deep Water Baptist

I said, "Uncle Versie, you have asked me to go talk to Newgene Ledbetter. What is the problem?"

He said, "Jerry, you know I'm a deep water Baptist. Newgene has done married a young Methodist girl, and they believe in sprinkling. It's hard for me to receive her into my home. I've told Newgene I wanted her baptized proper."

I said, "Uncle Versie, I think you're wrong. I love you, but that girl's got the right to be baptized like she wants to."

He said, "Jerry, them Methodists will do it either way. They'll put 'em under, or they'll put the water on the top of their head; and that girl's hardheaded. I want her baptized proper. She's my daughter-in-law."

I said, "Well, I'll go with you to talk to Newgene."

We went over to Newgene's house and there sat that precious little Methodist girl over there holding her Bible. Scared of old man Ledbetter because she hadn't been baptized proper, according to him.

Newgene said, "Papa, I have talked to some folks, and I'm willing to compromise with you. If me and that Methodist preacher and my wife go down to the river and she wades out in there knee deep . . ."

"No sir, that won't do."

"Well, Papa, what if we wade out in there hip deep . . ."

"That ain't no good. She just as well stayed on the bank."

Newgene said, "Well, Papa, what if we go out in there up to her Adam's apple?"

"You ain't talking to me. That's sinful."

"Well, Papa, what if we let her walk out in that river till there ain't nothing sticking out of the water but just the top of her head, will that do?"

He said, "No, that won't do."

Newgene said, "I knowed all the time it was just that spot on the top of your head that counted anyhow."

Clovis Gets a Job

Clovis Ledbetter, y'all remember him. He was the one that was downhearted all the time and never said a word until he was twenty-two years old. He didn't want to be Clovis Ledbetter; he wanted to be a log truck.

Everywhere he went, he went like he was a log truck. Grghhh . . . But after he got grown, he fell in love with a little girl and decided he'd commence to talkin'. He knew he had to get him a job, so he went to the Builders Mart store there in southwest Mississippi, and they recommended that he go to work for a local contractor.

Clovis Ledbetter got him a job. He said it was a construction job. He figured it was on the inside, so he didn't wear too many clothes. He was up four stories high, helping a bricklayer lay bricks. He was mixing the mortar and toting bricks to him. After about an hour, Clovis Ledbetter said, "I'm freezing to death. I got to go to the house and get me some more clothes."

The man said, "You can't leave. You're the only labor I've got. Get to work!"

He said, "Well, I'm freezing."

The bricklayer said, "I tell you what you do: get two of them strings over there and tie the bottom part of your britches leg as tight as you can to your boots, and then undo the two buttons on the side of your overall britches and yonder's a pile of stuff over there—Johns Manville fiberglass and Owens Corning fiberglass. You go over and just pick you out whichever one of them you want, or mix them up, and ram that fiberglass down in your britches leg. Pack it down there good. Get it all down in your stride. And then, Clovis, undo the bib of your overalls and take some of that pretty pink fiberglass and wrap it around your body, and then put the overalls back over it. You'll be warm!"

Clovis done that good, just like he was told. In about ten minutes the bricklayer said, "How you feeling?"

He said, "I'm burning up. This stuff's eating me alive!"

Clovis pulled off them overalls and slung all that stuff out of 'em, turned them wrong side outwards, and slipped them back on. And just as he hit the ground, he hollered, "What can I do for this?"

That bricklayer said, "Put alcohol on it."

Clovis Goes to Court

Clovis Ledbetter was fat. I growed up with Clovis. He was one of my dearest friends. He was Marcel Ledbetter's youngest brother. Clovis Ledbetter loved to eat so well, he'd just steal a chicken or a goat. One time he got arrested for stealing a sheep, and they put him in jail.

There he was behind bars, and one of them lawyers went to him and said, "Clovis, you in here, son. They done caught you. Ain't no way you can get out of jail unless you get a good lawyer like me to represent you. I can get you out for fifty dollars."

Clovis said, "Man, I ain't got no fifty dollars."

He said, "Well, you can work it out for me. Come over to my place and cut the grass and all that kind of business."

Clovis said, "All right. I shore don't want to go to Parchman penitentiary."

So, they done got Clovis Ledbetter in the courtroom to have the trial. The lawyer told him, "Now, Clovis, whatever you do, you do exactly like I tell you. I'm gonna get you out of this, but you've got to do like I tell you in the courtroom."

Now this was a smart lawyer—fancy fellow. He had a hairdo looked like a milking machine had been sucking on it. He instructed Clovis, and the district attorney got up and said, "Mr. Clovis Ledbetter, didn't you, on the night of so and so, steal a sheep?"

Clovis said, "Baa! Baa!"

He asked him another question and Clovis said, "Baa!"

The judge looked down at Clovis and said, "You answer that man's questions. What do you mean doing that?"

Clovis looked at the judge and said, "Baaaa!"

The judge took that hammer and hit the desk, and said, "Get that idiot out of here. He's crazy. Case dismissed."

Well, the next day the lawyer went and hunted up Clovis. He

wanted his fifty dollars. And Clovis looked at him and said, "Baa! Baaaa!"

Clovis the Constable

Clovis Ledbetter had him a job being a constable. Him and the town marshall, late every evening, would walk the railroad tracks and run them hobos off that'd be riding them trains.

Well, this particular late afternoon the freight train pulled in. They got on down to the end of the freight train and there sat a fellow on the coupling poles, between the main train and the caboose. He didn't look like no average hobo. He was six feet tall, weighed about 200 pounds—good looking fellow. They said, "Sir, it's against the law for you to be riding the train. We done caught you. Put your hands out. We're going to handcuff you and take you to jail."

This fellow said, "Mr. Constable, wait a minute. I want to tell you something. My mama was the finest godly Christian woman I've ever known in my life, and she's done gone home to heaven. My daddy was the meanest scoundrel I have ever known in my life, and I'm sure he's in hell. I'm gonna tell you one thing, if I don't get to ride this train to the end of the line to see my sister where she lives, I'm fixing to join either my mama or my daddy tonight."

Clovis Ledbetter sized him up pretty good, looked at the town marshall, and said, "Sir, anybody that wants to see their sister that bad, oughta be allowed to ride the train to the end of the line."

Claude and the Game Warden

I went to see Marcel Ledbetter the other day. His brother Claude was the only one in the community catching any fish. Other folks was going, and they wasn't catching nothing. Old Claude Ledbetter, he'd come in with a pickup truck loaded down.

So the state game and fish commission of Mississippi decided they'd go fishing with Claude, just see how he was catching them. Claude had told them—he popped off and said, "Y'all don't know how to do it. Y'all just ought to go with me and watch me."

Well, the game warden got up in the boat with him, and they took off out in the middle of the river. The game warden said, "All right, Claude, I'm gonna see how you catching all these fish when can't nobody else catch none." Claude raised the lid on the boat seat and got a big long stick of dynamite, lit the fuse on it, let it go down to kind of short, and drawed back and chunked it. Boom!

Them big catfish come turning their belly up, whipping it up out of that water, and Claude was just getting them by the tub full. The game warden said, "Boy, that's against the law. You can't do that. Don't you know you're breaking the law?"

Claude had done lit another big stick of dynamite, handed it to the game warden, and it was going, Shooosh! The game warden said, "You idiot, this is against the law, you can't do this."

Claude said, "You gonna sit there and argue, or *fish?*"

Double First Cousin

I want to introduce to you Vernell Ledbetter. Vernell is a double first cousin to Ardell, Burnell, Raynell, W.L., Lanell, Odell, Udell, Marcel, Claude, Newgene, and Clovis. Vernell Ledbetter was a different set, but he was a double first cousin cause his daddy was a brother to Uncle Versie, and his mama was a sister to Aunt Pet. Vernell Ledbetter was a smart aleck. He knew everything. He was scared to get around Marcel, 'cause Marcel would whip him just for being so smart-alecky.

Vernell would argue with a sign post. One day Vernell was at the Greyhound bus station in McComb, Mississippi, going to Jackson, our capital city. He bought his ticket, and he went off over yonder in the corner where they had some of them games, and where you could put money in a machine and get coffee, or put money in a machine and get cold pop. He was wandering around back there waiting for his bus, and he saw this machine that said "Put in a quarter," and the machine would tell you your name, how much you weigh, and where you going.

Vernell said, "That's impossible. That's a gyp. I ought to go up there and cuss out that fellow at the desk. He knows this is a gyp. But I'm gonna put a quarter in here, and if it don't do what it says, they fixing to hear from me. I'll call my lawyer."

He put the quarter in there and a little old card come slipping out a little slot, and it said: "Your name is Vernell Ledbetter, you're six feet tall, you weigh 178 pounds, and you're riding a bus to Jackson, Mississippi."

"Hoo!" he said. "That fellow put that information in some kind of computer thing and then put it in that machine. Had to!"

So, he went up there and got on the fellow and he said, "I didn't even know your name. You take that up with that machine and leave me alone."

Vernell went back up there and put in another quarter, and said, "I bet it don't do it this time."

The card come slipping out, "Your name is Vernell Ledbetter, you're six feet tall, you weigh 178 pounds, and you're riding the bus to Jackson, Mississippi."

Well, it was just more than he could stand. He finally decided to put one more quarter in it. He put the quarter in there and a card eased out, said, "Your name is Vernell Ledbetter, you're six feet tall, you weigh 178 pounds, and you have missed your bus to Jackson, Mississippi."

The New Baby

Vernell Ledbetter always said the wrong thing wherever he went. His mama was whippin' him all the time. There was a new baby born in the community and Vernell's mama hadn't been to see it, and she knew she had to go. The baby was about two months old, and it was kinfolks.

So one Sunday afternoon after church Vernell's mama got him ready and they walked over to the neighbor's. On the way over there she said, "Boy, if you open your cotton-pickin' mouth and say one bad thing, I'm gonna whip you all the way back home. Now let me explain to you on the front, this baby was born without no ears. If you mention it or even stare at that baby's head, I'm gonna knock you into the middle of next week. Do you understand?"

"Yes, ma'am."

When they got over there, Mrs. Ledbetter said, "What a beautiful baby. Oh! Ain't it precious. Beautiful little boy. Look at them big sturdy shoulders. Just look at them arms."

The boy's mother was so proud. "Yes, he is healthy."

Mrs. Ledbetter went on and on. "Look at them fine feet and them sturdy legs."

The mother said, "Yes, he is fine, isn't he?"

Mrs. Ledbetter went on: "Look at them big beautiful blue eyes, aren't they pretty."

The mother replied, "Yes, and he has 20/20 vision."

Vernell said, "It's a good thing, 'cause he ain't never gonna be able to wear glasses."

Last Rites

I done met my old buddy, Reverend Sam McAlwee. Brother Sam's been a good preacher forever. But the other day he was to preach a funeral, and he had a flat tire. He opened up the trunk of his car and got them old turkey huntin' coveralls and laid down there in the red dirt. He finally got his jack up, fixed the flat, brushed himself off, and rushed to the church. But there wasn't anybody there.

He went running in the church and there were two or three folks there. He said, "Is the funeral over?"

One said, "Well, they gone is all I know."

He said, "Well, what direction did they go in? Where's the graveyard?"

"Well, that was Aunt Hattie Simmons, and she growed up in the Oak Grove community out yonder. I'm shore they taking her to the Oak Grove Cemetery."

Well, he took off in boiling dust, scratching off, went rushing out there. He saw a graveyard, and way up on the hill past the graveyard there was two fellows throwing dirt in a hole. He run up there and jumped out of the car, looked down in the hole and said, "Well, I just as well say something. I done missed preaching the poor old soul's funeral."

He said, "Ashes to ashes, dust to dust. We will remember this beautiful lady the rest of our lives. Amen."

He got in his car and drove off. Udell and Vernell Ledbetter was leaning on the shovel handles. They watched him drive off. Udell looked at Vernell and he said, "You know, that's the strangest words I ever heard anybody say over a septic tank."

Railroad Man

I growed up right outside a railroad town. One day the local was coming up from New Orleans and stopped in Chatawa, Mississippi, loaded everything on, and got ready to pull back on the main track. The engine wouldn't crank. They sent to McComb where they have a roundhouse and they know all about engines. The top dog come down there, his assistant dog come down there, and assistant to that dog come down to Chatawa. They went to looking and fumbling and turning knobs and bolts and screws and electrical things, and it wouldn't crank.

By now a crowd had gathered. One old boy popped off: "I tell you one thing, old man Claymore Ledbetter could crank it. He worked for the railroad for fifty years before he retired. He knows more about an engine than anybody."

Well, the superintendent of the shop up there in McComb said, "Send and get him."

In just a few minutes they'd done fetched old man Claymore Ledbetter. He rubbed that engine, walked around it and looked at it, and said, "Who's the strongest boy in this group?"

They said, "Newgene Ledbetter, standing right over there."

He said, "Well go over there to the hardware and get him a sixteen-pound sledge hammer."

They got the sledge hammer and come back. Old man Claymore Ledbetter took a big old chalk and marked an X on the side of that engine. He said, "Newgene, hit that spot right there just as hard as you can."

Well, Newgene drawed back, and wham! That engine kicked off and began running like a sewing machine. Everybody applauded.

The big dog from the IC railroad shop said, "Sir, what do I owe you?"

Old man Claymore Ledbetter said, "One hundred dollars."

"A hundred dollars? How did you come to that conclusion?"

He said, "Well, give that boy that slung that sledge hammer a dollar for hitting the engine with the sledge hammer, and give me ninety-nine dollars for knowing where to hit the thing."

Public School Music Class

I took public school music at East Fork Consolidated High School. That was the only mandatory course we had in the whole school system. You didn't have no choice; you had to take it. Miss Minnie Lee Stone was our teacher, and whenever she knocked on the door and come in, it didn't make no difference what course you was a studying, you shut them books up and paid attention to her.

One day she entered the ninth grade class. Me and Marcell Ledbetter, his younger brother Claude, Ardell, and Burnell, Wilma Nell and Raynell, and Christine and W.L., and Sonny made up that class. Miss Minnie Lee Stone come walking in and she had two younguns with her a-totin' pasteboard boxes what had public school instruments in them. We was going to be members of the public school band. If you acted real nice she would let you whip them sticks together, and if you was good for two class meetings hand running, you could whop that tambourine. And if you was real good, you could hold that little triangle and take that little steel bar and tinkie, tinkie, tink on that triangle. Now, brother, if you could tinkie, tinkie, tink on that triangle, that was the leading instrument in the public school band.

This particular day she was all excited. Miss Minnie Lee Stone said, "Class, you know I have always regretted very much that none of y'all have never heard no world-renowned musician, but Mr. Dellsey, what's a world-famous piano player, is coming to McComb to visit his mama. I have written to him, and he is coming to East Fork and play for the chapel program, and y'all are gonna get to hear a world-renowned piano player."

The day he showed up, they made all of us go into the main big room where the piano was. They roped off the public school music group—made us sit as a group. Miss Minnie Lee Stone explained to us that this here Mr. Dellsey was going to be playing one of them concerto overtures what he had been playing in the minors—or for the minors, one or the other. I remember distinctly, them minors was involved in it one way or the other.

She said, "Class, if you will pay attention to this great artist, you can see in story form what it is he's playing."

And we listened real good.

Now, folks, that ain't the first time he'd ever played one of them pianos. Oh, he could forevermore whip up on a piano. Ever now and then he'd forget what piece it was he was playing and he'd just freeze, but in a second or two he'd think of it, and, brother, he would take off one more time.

Soon as he got done playing, they dismissed everybody except that group what was roped off. Miss Minnie Lee Stone had started squalling. It had done got to her. She was squalling and saying, "Class, wasn't that wonderful? Now, tell the teacher, what did you see? Some of you girls, what did you see?"

Christine throwed her hand up.

"Yes, Christine, what did you see?"

"Oh, Miss Minnie Lee, I saw a little deer running through the woods."

"Oh, marvelous, Christine. Wonderful, wonderful. You thrill me to death!"

"Wilma Nell, what did you see?"

Wilma Nell jumped up and said, "Oh, Miss Minnie Lee, I saw the little deer take a drink out of the bubbling brook while the water was pouring over the dam."

"Oh, God bless you, Wilma Nell! I'm so proud of this class. Let's hear from some of you boys."

"Claude Ledbetter, what did you see? Claude?"

Claude rammed both hands in his overall pockets, up to his elbows. He commenced to squirming and rubbing his bare feet on the floor. He spun all the way around in the desk—the desks weren't anchored to the floor at East Fork School.

"I ain't gonna lie about it. I ain't seen nothing, but I heard that dam when it busted."

Wooden Leg

I am a country boy, and my brother told me a story the other day down in Amite County about when he went out visiting with a feed salesman. He called on Uncle Ronnie Ledbetter. When he got out to Uncle Ronnie Ledbetter's, my brother like to had a heart attack. There was a hog out there in a pen with a wooden peg leg.

My brother Sonny said, "Uncle Ronnie, what in the world is that hog doing with a wooden peg leg? Why has he got a peg leg?"

Uncle Ronnie said, "Sonny, that's the most wonderful hog in the world. My house was burning about a year ago, and that hog rescued the baby, got him out and saved his life. We love that hog; he's just like a member of our family. A year before that, a little boy was drowning down at the baptizing hole in the river, and that hog jumped in that river and grabbed him and rescued him. That hog's just like a member of my family! We love that hog!"

Sonny said, "Yeah, but you still ain't told me why he's got a wooden leg."

Uncle Ronnie said, "Sonny, you just don't eat a hog that wonderful but one ham at a time."

ME AND MARCEL

You know money was real short when me and Marcel was growing up. We was wanting to get us enough money to go see a Tarzan picture show. We caught a bunch of raccoons and sent the hides off to Sears and Roebuck.

Wanna Buy a Possum?

You know money was real short when me and Marcel Ledbetter was growing up. We was wanting to get us enough money to go see a Tarzan picture show. We caught a bunch of raccoons and sent the hides off to Sears and Roebuck, but the price dropped, and when we got our check, it was for a dime. That's all they brought.

So, we decided we'd take to the woods with our possum dog and just sell possums for folks to eat.

We were in the Johnson Station community one night out up north of the railroad where they had a lot of persimmon trees. We were possum hunting. About that time I heard the big freight train coming. Marcel broke and run with his lantern, put his red bandanna around that light where it would make it bright red; he stood straddle of the railroad track, and went to waving that lantern, flagging that freight train.

"Marcelllll!" He kept flagging that train.

Man, a hundred-car banana train squeaked to a halt. The engineer and the fireman jumped off and asked, "What kind of emergency do we have here?"

Marcel said, "I wanted to see if y'all wanted to buy a possum."

The man said, "You idiot, you mean to tell me that you have done stopped a hundred-car banana train, seeing if we wanted to buy a possum? You must be an idiot. But I like possum, and inasmuch as we have stopped, what do you want for him?"

Marcel said, "We ain't caught him yet, just wanted to see if you wanted one."

Marcel and the City Fellow

One day, me and Marcel Ledbetter was laying by a patch of corn. We had throwed some whippoorwill peas down in the water furrow, where that old Sutton spring-tooth harrow would roll them peas around. They would come up and we could have us some fall peas to eat. This fellow come driving up in one of them A-model cars. He jumped out and said, "Hey, boy."
Marcel said, "You talkin' to me?"
He said, "Yeah."
Marcel said, "Whoa, Della. What you want, city fellow?"
He said, "These rows you plowing here, they sure are crooked."
Marcel Ledbetter said, "You can grow just as much corn on a crooked row as you can on a straight one."
The fellow said, "Well, the corn shore is yellow."
Marcel said, "We planted yellow corn."
The fellow said, "Well, there ain't very much between you and a fool, is it?"
Marcel said, "Nothing but a fence."

Play Pretties

When I was a boy we didn't have no toys. We called 'em play pretties. The most affluent youngun was the one that had the most empty Prince Albert tobacco cans.
I've rolled an old casing—folks call 'em tires now—a thousand miles down the dirt road. Sometimes we'd get up in it, hunker

down, put our head up there, scrunch down in it, and roll down the hill. Sometimes you'd beat the tire to the bottom of the hill!

Me and Marcel Ledbetter went hunting us an old car tire one day. We went up to an old junk yard. The man running it, he wasn't too bright. He'd spent three terms in the third grade—Hoover, Truman and Roosevelt. But we thought he'd give us a used tire if he had one. We got to looking and we saw an A-model roadster. "Looka there! Man, ain't that a pretty thing!"

He said, "Ain't no account. We done took all the parts off of it we can use. Ain't even no motor in it. If y'all can get them old tires patched up and push it out of here, I'll give it to you."

Me and Marcel pushed that sucker to my house, put it between the smokehouse and a big old fig tree. We'd sit out there in it and we'd "play-like." We'd drive down to New Orleans, come back up through Slidell, and sometimes we'd come up the other highway through Columbia and Hattiesburg. Ah, we was "good roading it" in our Model A roadster.

One day we decided we'd push it out there on Highway 24. Marcel was driving. We was on the gravel road, just sitting there, but we were "playing like." We was just south of Chicago when the road grader come along. Mr. Conway on the road grader jumped off, and said, "Boys, what's the matter? Your car won't crank?"

Marcel said, "Naw, sir, it won't crank."

He said, "Well, let me see if my bumper on this road grader matches, and I'll give you a push."

"We sure would appreciate it if you would push us."

Well, the bumper just happened to match. I didn't care if it had been a foot off. He eased up and I jumped in the car, and he got up just as fast as that road grader would go. We went about a quarter of a mile. He stopped and jumped off, and said, "What happened?"

Marcel said, "It didn't hit a lick."

The man said, "Well, I didn't push you fast enough." He flagged down one of them highway trucks. He said, "Look, we fixing to get into the Amite County river bottom now. This river bottom is about three miles across here and kinda flat. Get them boys up to about forty-five to fifty-five miles an hour and that thing'll crank."

Well, man, we got to going, rolling up the dust, and Marcel was doing it! Oh, he was steering, having a good time. Stopped after about three miles and the man got out of the truck and said, "Did it crank?"

Marcel said, "Naw, sir, didn't hit a lick."

The man said, "We got to figure out another way to crank it."

Marcel said, "It ain't gonna crank."

The man said, "What do you mean, it ain't gonna crank?"

Marcel said, "It ain't got no motor in it."

Marcel's Tongue

Me and Marcel Ledbetter was cleaning out a smokehouse one day. (That's where we smoked our meat.) He stood on a block of wood and reached way up on the top shelf, and there were some tin cans up there that had some fish hooks in them—some Luzianne gallon coffee buckets. They were rusty, and Marcel opened one of them. He saw the old fish hooks in there, and he sat it down on the stump.

Me and him was eating a raw sweet potato—that's good when you are hungry. About that time he kicked that stump over. He fell, and his chin hit the bottom of that Luzianne coffee can. He scrounched his mouth up, and blood was coming out of his mouth.

Aunt Pet Ledbetter was washing clothes on a rub-board right there by the front of that smokehouse, and she come running. She rolled him over, and he opened his mouth, and that piece of sweet potato came out on the ground. A big old Rhode Island red rooster run and grabbed it and took off running.

Aunt Pat yelled, "Come quick, a rooster's got Marcel's tongue."

Marcel's Plantation

Me and Marcel was in the barber shop one day. We had done walked ten miles to get there and saved enough money to get our hair cut. The barber cut it just as long as the hair lasted—just cut it all off, 'cause we couldn't afford to get one every other month.

We was sitting in there and a fellow come walking in with a big Texas hat on. He was a driller, hunting oil. He said, "Barber, do you have a shoeshine boy?"

"Shoeshine? Man, you crazy? Everybody in these parts shines their own shoes, them that's got shoes. We don't have no shoeshine boy."

Well, he talked ugly about how sorry "this hick community is. Don't have no shoeshine boy." He looked over at me and Marcel, we was sitting there barefooted. He said, "You two country boys there, y'all oughta shine shoes."

Marcel said, "I don't know how."

He said, "I growed up on a big ranch. I'm sure you country boys don't know nothing about that."

Marcel was just sitting there festering. He didn't like for nobody to look down on him. He said, "I growed up on a big plantation myself. Growing up on it right now. We got a fancy, beautiful plantation."

The man said, "Oh? What kind?"

He said, "A tea and fruit plantation."

"Oh? What kind of tea and fruit?"

Marcel said, "Sassafras and persimmon."

The Devil

East of Liberty, Mississippi, there is a little town called Gloster, and there's some pretty girls living in Gloster. One of my old buddies had a '37 Ford, and one Saturday afternoon, kinda late, we decided we would drive over to Gloster and see if we could get some of them girls to drive up and down Main Street with us. Well, we got over there, and them girls' mamas wouldn't let them get in the car with us. "But y'all can ride in the cars with them," she said. So, I got in one car and Marcel Ledbetter got in the other, and we're dragging Main Street—here we go.

Right after dark them girls said, "Well, we got to go to the house. Y'all get out." So, I got out of the car and walked down there to where we had that '37 Ford parked. I looked, and the moon had come up, and I could see Marcel laying down on the front floor board, shaking—just shaking! The car window was down, and I eased my head in and said, "Marcel! What in the world is wrong with you?"

He said, "I knew we shouldn'ta come down here. We done done wrong. We're sinning. The devil is after us!"

I said, "What do you mean the devil is after us?"

He said, "He is sitting in the back seat."

I looked around there and I saw two horns, two eyes, and whiskers. I said, "OOOeee! What do you mean?"

When I said that, something come out over that front seat, through the window, and knocked me down. Like to have scared me to death!

Some jealous boys had done shut a billy goat up on the back seat of our car!

Ox Pullin' Contest

When I was a boy growing up, everybody had an ox. Every family had some oxen; they logged with oxen. I've seen 'em coming out of the woods with great big yokes of oxen, pulling them logs, and they was popping their whips. We had us one old ox; we couldn't afford a pair of 'em.

They would have pulling contests all over the country. One day they were going to have a pulling contest in Liberty, Mississippi. Hey, we wanted to have this pulling contest at Liberty, and we wanted to enter it. But it was going to be a *team* of oxen. So, we went to a neighbor and we said, "Hey, you ain't got but one ox and we got one, why don't we enter them as a team at the ox pulling contest at Liberty?"

They said, "That'll be fine. But he's busy every day. We can't work our ox out, so you'll have to work out your ox some other way."

Marcel said, "Hook me up with the ox."

Marcel Ledbetter, he hunkered down and they yoked him in. He was hooked up with Old Buck, and he was going to teach Old Buck to work double. They were going to pull around there in the pasture a little bit. My brother, Sonny, was driving them, and he said, "Come up, Buck!"

Buck didn't budge. "Oh, Buck, come up!"

Sonny popped him right good, and buckity, buckity, buck, Buck run away—dragging Marcel Ledbetter across that pasture, down a ditch, through a creek. Buck cut through a bunch of sawbriars, and drug Marcel through a gravel pit. They finally hemmed Old Buck up in the corner of the pasture, and everybody eased up there.

They said, "Whoa, Old Buck, whoa Buck" and started to unhook Marcel.

Marcel said, "Don't unhook me; unhook Buck. I'll stand by myself!"

Our First Banana

Me and Marcel Ledbetter joined the navy together. We caught that fast train and we took off. I had never left my mama in my life. I was seventeen years old. We were homesick in about fifty-five seconds.

About three hours later a man came walking down the aisle of the train, had a basket in each hand, wearing a little white coat and cap. He said, "Apples, oranges, bananas. Apples, oranges, bananas. Get your apples, oranges, and bananas."

I said, "Marcel, what is a banana?"

He said, "I don't have no idea. I got a apple and a orange one Christmas, but I ain't never ever seen or heard of no banana."

I said, "Me neither." I called, "Hey fellow, what's them bananas?"

He said, "Two for a nickel."

I said, "Give me two of 'em. How you eat 'em?"

He said, "Peel 'em. Pull that yellow part off it."

Marcel hung his fingernails in that banana peeling and snatched it off, scooped him out a handful of that banana and popped it up in his mouth. About that time the train entered a tunnel. The railroad car got jet black dark.

Marcel said, "Whooo! Jerry, Jerry!"

I said, "What?"

He said, "Have you et your banana yet?"

I said, "Nah."

He said, "Well, don't. I took one bite of mine and went stone blind."

Civil War

I got to boot camp at Camp Perry, Virginia, and they put me and Marcel to sweeping the floor in a gymnasium with a big old broom. We come sweeping down through there, and two fellows sittin' over there was listening to me and Marcel talking. They said, "Where are you fellows from? Maybe you'd like to tell us who won the Civil War."

Marcel Ledbetter, all in one motion with that broom, broke it over that fellow's head and said, "The Civil War ain't over."

Marcel's Talking Chain Saw

Marcel didn't like school *none*. He didn't like them teachers, and he didn't like them books. Well, Uncle Versie made him stay in school till he was old enough to get his driver's license, and then bought him a secondhand pulpwood truck. Marcel quit school and went to hauling pulpwood.

Now, Marcel had loaded up his pulpwood truck and had took a load out to McComb and had unloaded it out there on the big boxcar what was going to the paper company. He was driving back out to East Fork community where he lived. It was in the hot of the evening just before sundown, and that sun was staring right in the face.

Now, Amite County is dry. The people are dry, and they had never voted for no kind of alcohol beverage. If you wanted to get a cool one, you had to ride over to the county line where they got a joint.

Marcel was coming along there. He'd had fine Christian teaching; he knowed better than to buy any of them cool beers. But he knew also they had them big Nehi bellywashers, and they was cold. And he wanted one of them so bad. He eased his old pulpwood truck off the paved highway.

Now, all he had on between him and the Lord was just a pair of overalls. He was barefooted and just his overalls on—that's all. He did have the bottom buttons on the side buttoned, but the top buttons was flopping.

He put his truck down in neutral, and he pulled the emergency brake up. Then he eased up to this tavern, and he looked through the screen door and said, "Hey!"

The man behind the counter asked him, "What you want?"

He said, "Would you hand me a cold soda water?"

"You better get away from that door! Go get you a shirt on; go get you some clothes. We don't want the likes of you in here."

"I ain't coming in. All I want you to do is hand me a cold soda water through the door. I'll pay you for it and pay you for the old bottle, and I'll drink it while I'm driving home."

There was four fellows sitting around a table there playing this booray card game, and one of them said, "Didn't you hear him tell you to get away from that door, you redneck?"

Pore old Marcel, walking on them gravels out there, went back to his truck and reached over in the toolbox and brought out one of them lightweight McCullough chain saws. He reached down and took ahold of that saw. *Waghhhh!! Waghhhh! Waghhh!!* He walked up to the door of that beer joint, and he just stuck the snout of that thing through the screen door. *Whaw! Whoommm!* He reamed him out a hole in that screen door, and he eased it over to the side and it hung in that screen door. *Whappp! Awhupp! Whap!* And he held it out up over his head, rived it up where all them screen wires and hinges and things would come loose from it . . . *Whop!* Then he stepped inside.

He raced the motor three or four times and slung that thing at a table and just cut off two legs of the table.

They gave Marcel the beer joint!!

Green Persimmon Wine

Now Marcel Ledbetter was my closest friend. He was a great fellow, and several people have asked me, "Did Marcel ever get into any trouble other than taking the chain saw and tearing up the beer joint?"

I'll have to admit that Marcel got into some trouble one time before that. Marcel and his younger brother Claude—to tell you about the trouble they got in—sneaked in early one morning to the East Fork Church and poured all of the grape juice out of the communion box and replaced it with green persimmon wine.

The next Lord's Day they served the Lord's Supper, and everybody in the church house partook. The preacher got up and said, "As is now our custom, we'll sing a song and go out."

They all had to stand and whistle the closing hymn.

Marcel's Race Horse

Marcel Ledbetter's done got him a race horse. He bought it making money hauling pulpwood. Got plumb excited racing the horse. Marcel come to see me, and I went to see the horse. It didn't look bad.

Marcel called me the other day and said, "Jerry, we're gonna race our horse this oncoming Saturday at Ferriday, Louisiana. We want you to come."

I couldn't get there, but Sunday morning bright and early I called Marcel Ledbetter. I said, "Marcel, did your racehorse win?"

He said, "Nah, but it took six of them to whip him."

Marcel Ledbetter Moving Company

Poor old Marcel, he's always tried to get in several kinds of businesses where he could make a profit and he wouldn't have to work so hard hauling pulpwood. He went into the moving business one time and got him a partner named James Lewis. Marcel Ledbetter Moving Company. He borrowed him some money, got him a few trucks, and one day the phone rang. "Mr. Ledbetter, will you move a piano for me?"

"Yes, ma'am."

They got to the house, and it was a three-story house with a big bay window on the second floor. She wanted them to move the piano out of there and down to the ground. Marcel got up there and got to checking, and it wasn't no way. After the piano was done moved up there, they'd fixed the door some way. Marcel couldn't wedge the piano down, and he didn't have enough folks to tote it.

Marcel said, "I know what I'll do."

He got him one of them two-by-sixes and went up there and nailed it on top of the house, stuck it out over the house, put him a block and tackle up there—one of them pulleys—brought the end down, and into the bay window. Then he tied it around the piano, real good.

James Lewis and the other hand went up there and was going to ease it out the window, and Marcel done wrapped the rope around his wrist down there on the sidewalk.

"All right, now, y'all be careful. Shove it out easy, and I'm gonna ease it down."

They eased it out the window, and just as it left the ledge, that thing started down and Marcel started up with the rope tied around his arm. He passed that piano about halfway up, and the piano hit the sidewalk—boom!—went into a thousand pieces. Splinters covered the whole street. Marcel's head hit that pulley up there. Boom! Down he come flat of his back, right down on all that busted piano. Knocked him unconscious.

Here comes James Lewis down the steps. He got down and he slapped Marcel. "Oh, speak to me!"

Marcel opened his eyes. He said, "Why should I speak to you? I just passed you twice up there and you didn't say nothing."

Employment Office

Speaking of hard times, Marcel Ledbetter called me.

I said, "How's the weather?"

He said, "It's done rained so much the white perch done eat up my gardens." He said, "Jerry, me and Ben DeLaughter ain't worked in two weeks. The woods is muddy, and we're just having a hard time."

I said, "Marcel, if you can't get a job, I'll help you. I'll send you a check every month. You're my friend and I love you."

He said, "I ain't asking for no handout. I done saved a little money. I was just wondering if it would be wrong if me and Ben DeLaughter went to the employment office and signed up."

I said, "Heck, no. It's for people like you. You been paying in all your life. You go down there. You put the best on you got, and you go." They dressed up and went to the employment office. Old Ben DeLaughter was suffering from static cling on his britches leg bad. They'd done hung tight to his ankles. Marcel could a-made a good "ring around the collar" commercial. They went in and the little lady hostess talked to them. They filled out the forms, and they sat down. In a few minutes, someone announced, "Ben DeLaughter, please."

Ben went down the aisle and back in there to one of them little private offices. That employment fellow said, "Sir, what is your occupation?"

Ben said, "I'm a pilot."

He said, "You ain't got a problem in the world. Beautiful! In fifteen days we'll have you a job. There's executives all over America looking for pilots."

Ben said, "Fine." And he left out.

"Mr. Marcel Ledbetter."

Marcel went in there and sat down with the fellow. He asked, "What is your occupation?"

Marcel said, "I'm a pulpwood cutter. I saw pulpwood for a living with this chain saw."

The man said, "Well, I'm sorry to tell you, but you're gonna have to sign up for unemployment. We got all the pulpwood cutters we need."

Marcel said, "I don't quite understand. My buddy just come out of here giggling and grinning. He said y'all was gonna have him a job in fifteen days."

"Yeah, but he has a skilled occupation: he's a pilot."

Marcel said, "That's right. He's as good as I ever saw. He does his job as good as anybody I ever worked with, but he can't work unless I work. I got to saw up pulpwood before he can pile it."

Marcel the Truck Driver

Marcel Ledbetter got him a job driving one of them trucks hauling cars—one of them deals they call transport haulers. He was up in that Mississippi Delta between Tunica and Clarksdale, Mississippi, the longest straight flat stretch of road in the world. He was getting it on, fifty-five miles an hour, late at night, and his lights went out.

He got the truck stopped before he wrecked and got to thinking, "What in the world am I gonna do?"

Marcel Ledbetter climbed up on the top of that cab, got up in the car what was hunkered over the top of the cab, with the lights sticking toward the road. Marcel got that door open and he turned them lights on, got back in the truck and cranked it up. Them car lights on that brand new car, up on top of his truck, was hitting the road way out yonder.

Marcel got back up to fifty-five miles an hour, and directly he met a vehicle coming toward him. That scoundrel took to the ditch and across through a cotton patch. Marcel got his truck stopped and run over there and said, "Friend, are you hurt?"

"Nah."

"What's wrong?"

He said, "I figured if that truck was as wide as it was tall, I better give him the whole highway."

Marcel and the Lady

One of the reasons I've loved Marcel Ledbetter all my life is because he ain't lazy. He was standing at the bus stop in McComb, Mississippi, the other morning, going to catch a bus out to the Fernwood Truck Terminal, where he could pick up his rig and drive a load of cars to Memphis, Tennessee.

Marcel was standing at the bus stop, and right in front of him was a girl female woman. She had the latest Pierre Cardin skirt for women on—real tight around the knees and real tight around the waist and big up through here. That bus pulled up and stopped, and that lady went to step up on that bus. That skirt caught her; she couldn't get her legs high enough to step up on the bottom step. So she reached around behind, got that zipper and unzipped the zipper a little bit. Then she tried to step again. Still too tight. She reached around the second time and unzipped it a little bit more, and it was still too tight. She reached around the third time and got hold of that zipper, and Marcel just eased his arms up under her, gently picked her up, and walked up on the bus and sat her down in a seat and said, "Woman, sit down! We'll be late to work!!"

The lady drawed back and slapped Marcel right in the face. She said, "You fresh thing. You get your hands off me."

Marcel said, "Fresh? Woman, you just unzipped my britches three times."

Is Anybody Up There?

Every now and then somebody will call Marcel and say, "Marcel, the woods are wet so you can't drive your pulpwood truck. How about taking a load of stuff for me?"

Marcel did that not too long ago. He went up in the mountains between here and Washington, D.C. He done sashayed around through North Carolina, and he was coming around a steep curve and lost control of the truck. Just as that thing went over a big ravine, Marcel jumped out and grabbed at a plant growing on the side of the mountain. He got ahold of a thing looked like a persimmon sprout. He hugged it and the root hung.

He looked down and saw that truck hit about 2,000 feet below in the gully. He got to shivering, he was so scared. He looked up and he couldn't climb that wall. He held on to that persimmon sprout; his knuckles was red, and he started praying. He remembered his faith.

"Oh Lord, help me! Oh Lord, I'm calling you hard. Lord, I need you some kind of bad awhile now. I need you! Oh Lord, is anybody up there?"

This voice said, "Marcel, have faith. Turn loose of the sprout."

"Is anybody else up there?"

Airport Goodbyes

Marcel Ledbetter had sent me word: "Jerry, I want to take a trip with you." He's my dearest and closest friend: Marcel Ledbetter. He met me at the Jackson, Mississippi, airport and said, "Jerry, I'm gonna fly to Boston, Massachusetts, with you."

Ahhh! I said, "All right, Marcel. I'll be glad to have you."

While we were standing there checking in on Delta Airlines, four people were standing over in the corner somewhat squalling and crying. A man was hugging an older woman and man and telling them goodbye. (That saddened me because I had had a few good-byes in my time, and I don't think it's fun.) Then the man left with the younger woman, and went over to the entrance to the snout what goes up to the airplane. He held this young woman, and they squalled and looked at one another. Then he, with his head down, disappeared up the runway. Then the three people joined one another and started squalling. Me and Marcel was squalling.

About that time the man stuck his head around from the opening of the passageway and waved at the three people. "See y'all Tuesday!"

Tater Rides the Moped

I checked on Marcel Ledbetter the other day. Marcel's still hauling pulpwood, and he's got a young boy named Tater—Tater Ledbetter—that helps him. Tater loves to go to the woodyard 'cause the man that is the manager owns one of them moped motorcycles. While they are unloading the pulpwood ole Tater rides the moped, but he's forbidden to take it outside the woodyard. This particular day Tater saw an opening in the fence and he give it a good kick, hard, and he went right on the road. He pulled up to the red light and stopped.

About that time a brand new Mercedes-Benz—one of them $70,000 ones—pulled out of a brand new showroom, whipped around, pulled on out, and stopped at the red light. The driver looked and there was Tater on the moped there. Tater leaned over and put his nose on the glass, trying to look in there. The driver of the Mercedes spooled the window down and Tater struck his head over in there and smelled them leather seats. Look at that dashboard! Looks like the console of a brand new cotton gin. Whooee! Looka heah, looka heah! "Sir, it's the most beautiful car I ever seen in my life!"

The fellow said, "Thank you, young man. Thank you very much."

Tater said, "How fast will it go?"

He said, "One hundred twenty."

OhHooHoooo! "One hundred twenty!!"

About that time the light changed. Tater swung back on the moped and the man took off—I mean really showed Tater how he could do it and just left tire tracks in the middle of the road.

The man's going along doing about ninety miles an hour and he sees a speck in his rearview mirror. The speck's getting closer and closer. About that time the speck passes him on the left-hand side. The man driving the Mercedes said, "Good gracious, that looked like that little ole boy on that moped. Ain't no way that could happen."

About that time he saw it coming back. It *was*, have mercy! "He done passed me twice!" He looked in the rearview mirror and here he comes again, right at the back of that Mercedes. And WHAM! He runs into the back bumper. The man slams on brakes, jumps out. Tater done bent the cooter shell on the back of that car, and there he was, laying down, in the middle of that moped, parts strewed everywhere.

The man saw he was breathing, and said, "Oh, son, I sure hope you are all right. Is there anything in the world that I can do for you?"

Tater said, "Yes sir, you can unhook my suspenders from your sideview mirror."

GOD'S GONNA
TAKE CARE OF ME

I've seen a heap of changes in how we do things in country churches. Years ago we had preachers who would come and preach trial sermons. And you always had a ruckus.

Temperance Meeting

In every county in rural America, there is a Pleasant Grove Church—godly folks. I went to a temperance meeting at Pleasant Grove, and they had a seventy-year-old woman up making a report and talking about old devilish alcohol. Everything bad that's ever happened in the world, she blamed it on alcohol.

I was kinda agreeing with her—I'm a teetotaller. I kinda step on it myself every now and then, but I'm for the truth, whatever the truth is. That lady was agin' alcohol, folks. She got done and she said, "I've made my report. Y'all got any questions?"

A young fellow got up back there—looked like a college student—and said, "Mrs. Anderson, how do you explain the fact that the Lord in the Word of God turned water into wine?"

She said, "Yes, and I'da thought a lot more of him if he hadn't a done that."

Here's Hope

I went to the revival at our church Monday night, and the preacher started a big ruckus in my church. We are traditionalists, since 1810. Women folks feed the preacher, and he eats before the evening service. Well, this preacher got there, and he decided he did not want to eat before he preached.

I remember when I first backed into show business, I went to a place and they said, "Mr. Clower, Porter Wagoner was here last year and he preferred to eat after the show, so we have decided that you didn't want to eat. Everybody's already eaten and maybe you can just get you something after the show." I said, "Well, the next time you want to find out about my eating habits, you check with me; don't check with Porter Wagoner. 'Cause you looking at a man that can eat right before the show, or I can eat during the show, or I can eat right after the show."

Well, this preacher throwed a fit. His enzymes did not function properly and so he had to eat after the service. The women didn't like it, but they fixed it where he could eat after the service.

Monday night he started off the revival. When he got done, a little boy come up to him out of the audience, walked up there and pulled him by the coat. The preacher turned around and smiled, and the little boy looked up and said, "You might as well've *et*."

The Baptizing

I heard about a preacher the other day who was in bad trouble in his church. He never preached about anything except baptizing. I mean folks had been there forever, and this preacher had been there three months, and they hadn't heard no sermon except on baptizing. They called him in and said, "Hey, we got to do something."

He said, "Well, I didn't know y'all felt that way. Here's the Bible. You pick out the text and I'll preach on whatever you pick out. Come on, let's get with it."

They said, "All right, here's the text, Matthew 3:10: 'And now also the axe is laid to the root of the trees.'"

He got up in the pulpit, he read that text, and said, "Amen. That's wonderful. They laid that axe at the root of the tree. The only reason anybody would lay an axe down at the root of a tree is to take the axe to cut down the tree, to dam up the creek, to get the water deep enough to have a baptizing."

Killin' Offense

I have been an active Southern Baptist Christian for fifty-one years. I've seen a heap of changes in how we do things in country churches. Years ago we had preachers who would come and preach trial sermons, and you would have four or five of them, and somebody would vote for each one of them. And you always had a ruckus. Now we select a pulpit search committee, and put five folks on it that only God could get to agree on anything. When them five hear a preacher, and come and say, "We done found one," we call him. That's the best way to do it.

I remember when I was a boy, a trial preacher showed up. He come walking down the aisle to preach, and just as he got to the second pew from the front, there sat our senior deacon, with a black and tan hound dog sitting right there by him in the church.

That preacher took his Bible and whipped his britches leg, and said, "Get out of here, you nasty scoundrel," and kicked the dog till everybody just lost their breath. Where I come from that's a killin' offense. You don't kick no dog.

"Well, the senior deacon'll kill him as soon as church is over."

The trial preacher went on preaching, got done, and got outside and everybody was just excited. They just knew there was gonna be a ruckus. The senior deacon walked up to the preacher that had just preached the trial sermon, and said, "Preacher, I want to thank you for kicking my dog out of the church."

"Oh?"

"Yeah. I wouldn't a-had my dog to hear that sermon for nothing in the world."

The Preacher's Water

We had a preacher in Yazoo City, Mississippi. He wasn't a real ordained preacher; he was a self-appointed preacher. He had done hisself up as being a preacher, and he acted sometimes, when he was out of the pulpit, not in a nice manner.

He was weaving down the road the other day, and the highway patrol took to him, stopped him. He spooled the window down, said, "What can I do for you, officer?"

He said, "You weaving like you drinking something."

"Oh, you know I wouldn't drink nothing."

He said, "What's that down there on that seat by your leg? What are you holding down there? There's a bottle in a sack down there."

The preacher said, "That's water, plain pure water."

The highway patrolman reached and got it, stuck his finger down in there, and licked his finger. He said, "That's wine!"

The fellow said, "Praise God, He's done it again!!"

Two Mean Brothers

There was two mean brothers, awful, low-down brothers, lived in this southern town. One of 'em died, and the other one went to the local preacher. He said, "When you preach my brother's funeral, you get up in the pulpit and call him a saint, and I'll give you a thousand dollars."

Well, they had the funeral. There lay the dead, mean man in the casket. Right over here on the front row was the mean brother what was paying the one thousand dollars if the preacher called the dead mean man a saint.

The preacher preached, and directly he said, "Ladies and gentlemen, this dead fellow was low-down, stinking. He could crawl under a snake's belly. Ah, he was a reprobate. He was nothing. But compared to his brother sitting right over here, this man was a saint."

The Dead Cat

Y'all heard about the lady what lost her cat and took the cat in a little casket up to a big church, and said, "I want you to bury my cat."

They run her off, said, "We ain't near about gonna do that."

She took it to another church, and they run her off. Then she took the cat to a Baptist church out on the edge of town and told the preacher she couldn't find nobody to hold a service for a dead cat.

The man talked to her bad. "How dare you think we would bury a cat."

She said, "Well, I'm frustrated, and I am prepared to give two thousand dollars to whoever holds a service for my cat."

And the preacher said, "Lady, why didn't you tell me your cat was a Baptist?"

The Pulpit Committee

Every now and then I feel like I run up on somebody that's so heavenly minded they ain't no earthly good. I had such a fellow to call me the other day.

"Brother Jerry, I represent the pulpit committee of my church. We're interested in your pastor, and we'd like very much to come and hear him preach. Brother Jerry, would it have any bearing on our friendship whatsoever if I brought a pulpit committee to hear your preacher?"

I said, "Fellow, what's wrong with you? You talking about the workings of the Holy Spirit. If the Lord wants my preacher to go to Arkansas, Jerry wants my preacher to go to Arkansas. Now if he leaves, I'm gonna cry, 'cause I love him. He's been here a long time. I know his wife and I know his younguns. But you come right on."

"Oh, beautiful, Jerry. We knew you'd have a Christian attitude. Now, Brother Jerry, how are you doing?"

I said, "I'm doing bad."

"Oh? What's the matter?"

I said, "I'm exhausted. I am exhausted!"

"Oh? Why are you so tired?"

I said, "I been raising money all day."

"Raising money? Oh, Brother Jerry, what's the project? What you raising the money for?"

I said, "To pay for this sex change operation my preacher is fixing to have."

God's Gonna Take Care of Me

Let me tell you a story about a flood in the Delta country. Civil defense folks pulled up to the front porch and there sat a farmer. The water was done up over his boots. The civil defense man in the boat said, "Oh, sir, it's projected and predicted that the dam is about to bust. Get in the boat, let me save you."

He said, "You go ahead, fellow, with your boat. God's gonna take care of me."

Five hours later the boat come back and the fellow was sitting up on the roof, hanging on to the chimney. Water was up over his belt buckle. The civil defense boat pulled up and the man said, "Oh, sir, get in the boat. The dam did bust. Ain't no hope for you. Get in the boat."

The man said, "Y'all go ahead. God's gonna take care of me."

About an hour later a helicopter flew over. The man is standing up on the chimney. That helicopter hovered down over him, and let that rope down. They had a bull horn. "Catch a hold of the rope! Sir, this is your last chance. Catch a hold of the rope."

The fellow said, "Go ahead. God's gonna take care of me."

Well, the scene shifts to heaven. The fellow is graveyard dead—drowned. The fellow looked at the Lord and said, "Lord, I'm disappointed. You said you was going to take care of me. I'm embarrassed."

The Lord said, "You dummy, I sent you two boats and a helicopter."

MAMA'S DEAL
AND OTHER
FAMILY MATTERS

I

. . . . f God give me the

ingredients and told me to make a woman, I

would make her exactly like my wife.

Mama's Deal

I was doing a syndicated talk show on national television in Philadelphia, Pennsylvania. I was sitting in the greenroom and a lady come walking in. I knew she was a lady as to how her dungarees was fitting her when she come walking in. There wasn't a vacant chair, and I got up and said, "Take this seat."

She said, "You sit down!!!"

Well, it shocked me. I said, "Darling, there's not a vacant seat. Would you take this chair?"

"YOU SIT DOWN!!!"

I said, "I ain't gonna do it!"

Pearl Bailey was on the show. She leaned over and said, "Jerry, that's one of the top women libbers in the world. She thinks you offered a chair just to aggravate her."

Nothing could be further from the truth. I said, "Lady, I didn't mean no harm. I was just trying to be courteous. I offered you a chair because that's the way my mama taught me to be. And if you don't like it, you go see my mama."

The lady said, "Before I'm through, I intend to liberate some phase of each and every woman's life in America."

I said, "Well, darling, I'm a former professional salesman. Would you allow me to give you a little bit of advice? You can catch more flies with sugar than you can vinegar. You're too mad about everything, and I just believe you'd get more cooperation if you just wasn't so hostile."

She said, "I can tell by the way you talk, your own wife needs liberating."

She just as well spit on me. And I'm praying, "Lord, don't let me grab this woman."

I said, "Lady, you gonna liberate my wife? You don't even know my wife."

I said, "You done jumped on the wrong fellow, there ain't a big-oted bone in my body. I been loving women ever since I found out I wasn't one. I been watching women standing side by side with men all my life doing the same work, making a third as much money, and I'm just as opposed to that as I am communism." I said, "I'm the only friend you got in the whole state of Mississippi, and you're making me mad. You gonna liberate my wife? You don't even know her.

"Let me tell you a little about my wife. Me and Mama growed up together. We walked down the aisle of an old country church to-gether. We publicly professed our faith in Christ together. We was baptized together. I never dated another girl. I never had another sweetheart. If God give me the ingredients and told me to make a woman, I would make her exactly like my wife. We got four head of younguns. We been married since August 15, 1947. And you gonna liberate Mama?"

I said, "Mama sleeps every morning until she gets ready to get up. And when she does get up, a lady walks back there to the bedroom and says, 'Mrs. Clower, you want to have your breakfast back here, or do you want to have breakfast in the breakfast room, or do you want to have breakfast on the patio?' And however Mama wants breakfast, that's the way Mama gets breakfast.

"Then when them afternoon TV shows start, Mama can watch them in three different locations in the house—laying down, lean-ing, or propped up. And not only that, but when Mama gets ready to go to the grocery store or to get her hair fixed, she goes in a brand new gold Lincoln Town Car."

I said, "Lady, Mama don't want you messing with the deal she's got."

My Katy Burns

Well, let me tell you about my Katy Burns. She sneaked up on me and Mama. Mama was forty-four years old when Katy was born.

My little Katy was driving with me the other day down Grand Avenue in Yazoo City, Mississippi. She was playing "grown-up"—she was five years old then. She had a pair of white gloves on and was laying on the floorboard of my Dodge pickup truck. She was was laying on the floorboard of my Dodge pickup truck. She was fixing them gloves on her fingers, and all of a sudden she screamed. I thought a wasp had stung her.

I said, "Darling, what is the matter?"

She said, "Daddy, if I had one more finger, I could count to eleven."

Wesley Trees the TV

I got a grandson three years old. He was sitting in the floor late one afternoon playing with his toys. My son was sitting in the den with him. The "Dolly Parton Show" was on the TV. Dolly Parton said, "Ladies and gentlemen, we're fixing to take a break, but we'll be right back with a singing grandmother."

Wesley got up, got him a seat on the couch, and he treed that TV set. Wesley's got the TV treed!

In a little bit when the commercials were over, Dolly came back on. She said, "Ladies and gentlemen, here is a singing grand-mother—Tammy Wynette!" The little fellow's lips started quivering, he started crying. Dolly had done lied to him. Oh! He was upset!

My son called me and told me what had happened. I said, "Bring Wesley to me this minute."

"Daddy, I can't."

I said, "You bring that boy to me. And the minute he gets here I'll make his grandmother sing."

Sonny and Rambo

I've often spoke of my brother, Sonny. My brother, Sonny, wears sixteen battle stars—he is a war hero. Ah, he's a good'un. He called me the other day, and he was real upset 'cause them terrorists had done killed a man aboard a ship and throwed him overboard.

I said, "Sonny, we gonna catch 'em."

He said, "We oughta bomb anybody that we think done it."

I said, "You can't do that."

It wasn't long, we done caught 'em, and I called my brother, Sonny, back. I said, "Sonny, ain't you glad four American navy jets has done whipped up beside one of them Egyptian jets and we done made him land, and them four terrorists are on there? We got 'em."

He said, "They oughta shot 'em down. Killed 'em in the air."

I said, "Sonny, you sound bad as Rambo."

He said, "I'm sick of hearing about Rambo. My grandson has been talking about Rambo: 'Rambo, Rambo!' I asked him, 'Who is Rambo?' And my grandson took me to the picture show and let me watch old Rambo."

I said, "Sonny, what'd you think about him?"

He said, "Jerry, I was in a pretty tough outfit when I fought a war. If Rambo had a been in my unit in the navy, he'd been a cook."

Tar Baby

You know where we growed up at Route Four, Liberty, Mississippi, there was a big construction job going on one time when they were building a new high school. They were putting a tar roof on the building.

There was a lady living close by who had sixteen younguns. She wasn't an old woman; she had one a year, just like a brood sow. I mean she had a bunch of younguns.

One day she lost one of her little children. She got to hunting him and come to find out he had fell in a fifty-gallon drum of that melted black tar up at the school house. She reached down and got him, picked him up, and then shoved him back down in there. She said, "Boy, it'd be a lot easier to have another one than to clean you up."

The Deacon's Son

I got a fishing buddy in my church, and he was telling me the other day he was having a problem with his boy. The boy came in and said, "Daddy, I'm old enough to get my driver's permit, and I want to get it. Then when I get my driver's license thirty days from now, I want a brand new car."

My deacon friend looked his son in the eye and said, "You are a good boy, but there's three things you're going to have to do before I buy you that car. You're going to have to read your Bible more every day. You're going to have to pull up your grades a little better than they are now, and you're going to have to get a haircut."

Well, the boy came back to his daddy about the time he was getting his driver's license, and he said, "Daddy, I'm ready for my car."

He said, "Son, I notice you are reading the Bible a lot more, you have pulled up your grades, but you do not have a haircut."

The boy said, "Daddy, I been thinking about that. John the Baptist, Moses, and Jesus all had long hair."

And the boy's daddy said, "Yeah, and they walked everywhere they went."

John Dunn

There was an old boy that I knew real well that needed a job. He heard they had work in New York City. He done saved him some money and got on the Greyhound bus and headed to New York, hunting work.

Well, there was a woman met him down at the bus station. God bless her, a dear lady, she thought New York was about the size of McComb, Mississippi. She didn't know how big it was; she really didn't. She was waiting there and this old boy got on the bus to go to New York, and she said, "Young man, I got a son left here three weeks ago. His name is John Dunn. When you get to New York, if you run into my son, would you please tell him to write to his mama? Please!"

Well, the old boy got to New York and got off the Greyhound bus and started down the street. He looked and saw a great big building, said "Dunn & Bradstreet." He said, "My soul, there's old Dunn right there."

He walked in the lobby of that big beautiful building, and there set a receptionist lady, and he said, "Y'all got a John here?"

"Yes, right straight down at the end of the hall."

This old boy walked down to the end of the hall, a door opened, and this fellow come walking out. He said, "Are you Dunn?"

He said, "Yes, I am."

He said, "Your mama said to write her a letter."

Cholesterol

My doctor is after me about my cholesterol level. I bet the idiot that discovered the cholesterol level is the same person that come up with the windchill factor. My mama's been cold ever since. Now they done come up with the heat index, just stuff to make us uncomfortable, us good old boys.

My doctor is on me bad about my cholesterol level, and I have decided that it's directly associated with who your mama and daddy was—bloodlines.

I got a buddy in Amite County, Mississippi, that's five foot tall, weighs 348 pounds. Every morning at breakfast he eats a settin' of eggs, six of them big old hog sausages, eight biscuits, and sawmill gravy poured over them, made out of hog lard and cow cream. And if he don't suck up all that gravy with them biscuits, he drinks what's left in the pitcher. His cholesterol count is 131.

My doctor's had me on a diet of broiled mockingbird for two months, and my cholesterol count is 250.

I think it all depends on who your mama and daddy is; that's what I think.

Elevator

I have moved from Yazoo City, Mississippi, to Amite County— Route 4, Liberty, Mississippi. After I got back to the old home place, I found out there is a grown adult man in that county that ain't never been out of Amite County. He's a logger, hard worker. He just chooses not to go nowhere. He logs and stays at the house.

Well, he had a boy who went off to college and got a pretty big job, and he bought the old man a satellite TV dish. The old man was watching the Nashville Network and saw Jerry Clower on the Grand Ole Opry.

He told his boy, "I can't stand it. I said I never would leave Amite County, but I want to go to the Grand Ole Opry and see Jerry."

The young man loaded up his papa and took him to Nashville. He was having a good time! They took him downtown to look at them tall buildings. That old man looked at them tall buildings until the roof of his mouth sunburned.

They went out and checked into the Opryland Hotel, got on the elevator, and the door shut. That old man braced himself. The elevator stopped on the second floor, the door opened, and the ugliest woman in Tennessee got on—I mean she would stop a Volvo. The door shut, and the elevator took off and stopped on the third floor. The elevator door opened, and this ugly woman got off. The door closed, but before the elevator moved, the door opened again, and a beautiful young lady, Miss Tennessee, walked on. The door shut.

The old man looked at his boy and said, "Son, we need to run your mama through this thing."

They Comin' Back

I ran into an old boy the other day and he said, "Jerry, I envy you. Your last child has done got out of school, and you and Mama are at the house by yourself."

My good buddy once said, "Life really begins when all your children leave home and the family dog dies."

This old boy told me, "Jerry, your last child's gone. I certainly look forward to my last child leaving home where I won't have any obligations, and me and Mama can live it up."

I said, "Yeah, they gonna leave home and you can live it up, but do it quickly because they comin' back. They're comin' back, and they're gonna bring more with 'em!"

SHOOT THIS THING!

The whole top of the tree was shaking. The dogs got to biting the bark of the tree and fighting one another underneath the tree.

"Knock him out, John."

A Coon Huntin' Story

Where I come from—Route 4, Liberty, Mississippi—is twelve miles west of McComb, Mississippi, sixty-five miles due northeast of Baton Rouge, Louisiana, and 116 miles due north of New Orleans, Louisiana. It was there that I first saw the light of day in Amite County, September 28, 1926. Now, as I grew up in that community the only extracurricular activities that we engaged in was to go coon huntin' or to revival meeting if we had our crop laid by. And that's all we did except work.

This particular time that I want to tell you about is one evening when we were going coon huntin'. We had a pack of hounds. When we went to the mill to get our corn ground up, we'd get some ground up for dog bread, and we'd get some ground for just regular corn meal for human consumption. This particular day we weren't too busy. All we'd done was just cut down a few fence rows, shucked and shelled some corn, went to mill, drew up some water because that was wash day, helped get the sow back what rooted out from under the netwire fence, sharpened two sticks of stove wood real sharp and pegged them down over the bottom wire of the fence where the hogs couldn't root out no more, and had a rat killing. If I'm lying, I'm dying!

Well, this particular day after we got through with the rat killin', I walked out on the front porch and I hollered, "Hooooo, oooooo," and them dogs come out from under the house barking. They knew we was going coon huntin'. I hollered again and my neighbor, way across the sage patch, hollered back. That meant "I'll meet you halfway."

We met in the middle of that sage patch and he had his dogs, Ole Brummy, Queen, and Spot. I had Tory, Little Red, and Ole Trailer. We went down into the swamp and we started hunting. Oh, we was having such a fine time. Caught four great biguns. Then I heard a racket and it scared me, and I whipped my carbide light, what I had wired to my cap, around there, and I was looking in the vicinity of where I heard the racket coming from. The beam of light hit a man right in the face, and it likened to have scared me slap to death, because we was hunting on this man's place.

I said, "Mr. Barron, is that you?"

He said, "Yes, Jerry. What are y'all doing?"

"We hunting."

"How many y'all caught?"

"Four great biguns."

He said, "Well, boys, I'm glad to see you. Y'all want to spend the rest of the evening hunting with me and John?"

Well, I looked and lo and behold there was John Eubanks, a man who lived on Mr. Barron's place. John Eubanks was a great American; he was a professional tree climber. He didn't believe (I'm telling you the truth) in shooting no coon out of no tree. It was against his upbringing. He taught us from birth, the day we were born, till the age we would keep listening to him, "Give everything a sporting chance. Whatever you do, give it a sporting chance." He'd a been a great conservationist today, if he were here.

John said, "Take a crosscut saw coon hunting with you. When you tree a coon, hold the dog and cut the tree down, or either climb the tree and make the coon jump in amongst the dogs. Give him a sporting chance." A lot of times we'd climb a tree and make a coon jump in amongst twenty dogs, but at least he had the option of whipping all them dogs and walking off if he wanted to. This was strictly left up to the coon.

So I said, "Mr. Barron, we'd be glad to go huntin' with you."

You know, he was a rich man. He had sold a lot of cotton during the First World War for a dollar a pound. He had some world-renowned dogs, and we hollered three or four times and they started hunting. We listened, and Ole Brummy—Ole Brummy didn't bark at nothing but a coon—had a deep voice, and when he cut down on him, it was a coon. Don't worry about no possum or no bobcats, Brummy was running a coon. Ole Trailer, and Ole Highball, and them famous dogs of Mr. Barron's kept right in there with them. And Ole John Eubanks would holler, "Hooooo! Speak to him!"

And my brother, Sonny, hollered, "Hoooo, look for him!"

Oh, it was beautiful! Now y'all get this picture. About that time they treed. We rushed down into the swamp, and there the dogs were, treed up the biggest sweet gum tree in all of the Amite River swamps. It was huge—you couldn't reach around this tree. There wasn't a limb on it for awhile. It was way up there. Huge tree.

I looked around at John, and I said, "John, I don't believe you can climb that tree."

And it hurt John's feelings. He pooched his lips out, got fighting mad. He said, "There ain't a tree in all these swamps that I can't climb."

He got his brogan shoes off and he eased up to that sweet gum tree. He hung his toenails in that bark, and he got his fingernails in there, and he kept easing up the tree, working his way to that bottom limb, and he finally got to it, and he started on up into this big tree.

"Knock him out, John-n-n!"

It won't be long! And John worked his way on up to the top of the tree. Whoo-oo! What a bigun! He reached around in his overalls and got that sharp stick and he drawed back and he punched the coon. But it wasn't a coon—it was a lynx! We called 'em "souped-up wildcats" in Amite County. That thing had great big tusks coming out of his mouth, and great big claws on the end of his feet; and people, that thing attacked John up in the top of that tree.

"Whaw! Ooooo!" You could hear John squalling.

"What's the matter with John?"

"I don't have no idea what in the world's happening to John!"

"Knock him out, John-n-n!"

"What in the world's happening to John?"

"Knock him out, John-n-n!"

"WOW! OOOO! This thing's killing me!"

The whole top of the tree was shaking. The dogs got to biting the bark of the tree and fighting one another underneath the tree, and I kicked 'em and said, "You dogs get away!"

"What's the matter with John?"

"Knock him out, John-n-n!"

"Yow-owooo! This thing's killing me!"

John knew that Mr. Barron toted a pistol in his belt to shoot snakes with. He kept hollering, "Ohhhh, shoot this thing! Have mercy, this thing's killing me! *Shoot this thing!*"

Mr. Barron said, "John, I can't shoot up in there. I might hit you."

John said, "Well, just shoot up in here amongst us. One of us has got to have some relief."

Coon Huntin' on TV

I really don't have time to go coon huntin' anymore. But I did go coon huntin' the other day. WTBS out of Atlanta done "Portrait of America" and they featured Mississippi, and they had old Jerry on there. These TV folks said, "We want to do a coon hunt. We'll bring our equipment and go down to the woods, and we will run the little raccoon."

My manager said to them, "Good gracious, I've heard Jerry talk about coon hunting enough. You may jump that scoundrel here, and across four bottoms, three brier patches, and two rivers, you may tree him."

"Gee, I didn't know that."

So I called old Tennessee Hennessy, my buddy in Yazoo County that's got the coon dogs, and I said, "Hey, let's set up a coon hunt and get a coon up in a tree where these dogs will run a little ways."

Well, y'all oughta seen these WTBS folks when they come down there with these two New York producers. We held these four coon hounds, and these hounds saw that coon go up that tree.

One of the producers said, "Hold the dogs. I'm going to put the camera on the dogs. When I tell you to release the dogs, you release them."

Well, I knew what was going to happen because the coon in the tree was right behind the Yankee with the TV camera. He said, "All right, I got a good shot of them; release the dogs."

Whahhh! They knocked him backwards. Dogs, everything, went all over him and the camera. He laid down on his back and shot that scene up that tree.

These two Yankee women, holding their long-tail dresses, running through the brier patch, said, "Which way did the raccoon go?"

Squirrel Huntin'

I got a grandson thirteen years old. His name is Jayree. He come to see me Thanksgiving Day, and he was real excited. He wanted to go squirrel huntin'. I told him he could go squirrel huntin' with my housekeeper's boy, Maceo, and they could go the following day, Friday.

I had to go to bed early that night, because I was booked Friday and Saturday. So, I went back and got in the bed. Jayree was so excited about he was going to get to go squirrel huntin' in the morning on his granddaddy's place. I was near about asleep, and I felt something snatching the cover.

I said, "Yeah?"

"Granddaddy, Granddaddy!"

I said, "Yeah?"

"Granddaddy!"

"That you, Jayree? What you want?"

He said, "Is seventy-five shells enough?"

Peg Leg

There's a beautiful story that my buddy, Jim Ed Brown, shared with me. You know we did "Nashville On the Road" for about seven years, and I love him. He's a dear friend of mine. Jim Ed Brown grew up around Pine Bluff, Arkansas, in a sawmill. His father owned the mill and he was one-legged—he had a peg leg—and he walked on that peg leg.

One day Jim Ed and his father was down at the deer camp and they was all out deer hunting. About the middle of the afternoon Mr. Brown came back to the deer camp and looked up Jim Ed and he said, "Son, I done messed up."

Jim Ed said, "Daddy, what did you do?"

His daddy said, "I mistakenly killed a doe."

Jim Ed said, "Well, you ain't got no problem. Just shut up about it."

He said, "Jim Ed, I want you to go down yonder in them woods and I want to show you where I killed that doe, and you drag that thing away from there."

Jim Ed said, "Papa, there's no need to do that."

The father said, "Jim Ed, you don't understand. My peg leg tracks are all around that thing."

Deer Huntin'

From Route 4, Liberty, where I live, to the Mississippi River, all the way through Liberty and Gloster, Mississippi, during deer huntin' season it's just like you swept the streets clean. Ghost towns. Everybody is huntin' deer. Well, I don't deer hunt because I didn't deer hunt when I was a boy. Well, there wasn't no deer. I kinda hunt what I hunted then—raccoons and squirrels and possums. Folks want me to go deer huntin' and turkey huntin', and I don't know how. But my grandchildren are into hunting. My grandson said, "Granddaddy, will you help me get equipped to go deer huntin'?"

I said, "Certainly. I love you. What do you need?" Well, he named off a 30.06, and a doolywahdo, and a whimdiddly and a 39.09432B. Oooooo! After I counselled with my banker, I said, "Yeah, I'll get you one of them rifles. I hope this is it."

"Oh, no, sir, I need a grunt."

I said, "Boy, you need a what?"

"A grunt! It's made by Strutt."

I said, "What does a grunt do?"

He said, "If you sound that old grunt, that old buck thinks he hears a doe, and here he comes."

I said, "You sure you doing this fair?"

He said, "Now, Granddaddy, I also need a scent."

"You need a what?" "A scent!" I said, "I know you ain't playing fair now."

He said, "Granddaddy, when you was much younger, didn't Grandmother put on some of that sweet-smelling stuff to attract your attention?"

I said, "She did. And she did attract my attention. In fact, she flung a craving on me." And I said, "Son, I sidled up as close to her as I could, but she didn't shoot me."

The First Deer

Now, if your grandchildren or your children are into deer huntin', explain to their mama and their grandma that when they kill their first deer, they stick their face down in the blood—put it all over them.

Now, don't forget to do that, because my grandson done took that grunt, and took that scent, and done took that rifle Thanksgiving afternoon. He stayed in the woods Friday and Saturday, and on Saturday he come back about four o'clock in the afternoon, busted through the front door. Whaaa! There was blood from his eyeballs down to his ankles. And he's running through my fancy new house headed down the hall hunting his grandmother.

Well, about the time I got through mouth-to-mouth resuscitating his grandmother, that boy was back in the woods hunting another deer.

Now, if I'd a-known that he'd been that happy killing a deer, I'd a bought a deer and let him shoot it.

Quail Huntin'

I was at the country store one time when I was a youngun, and Marcel Ledbetter had been quail huntin' all day. He come in about four o'clock in the evening and walked into the store. The man that owned the store said, "Marcel, did you kill any quail?"

Marcel said, "I killed sixteen."

A fellow sitting on a cracker barrel said, "I betcha shot 'em setting on the ground."

Marcel said, "Can they fly?"

Bird Huntin' at Uncle Versie's

I done met more folks out there in Hollywood. I was out there the other day and one of them MCA Records executives said, "Jerry, I sure would love to go bird hunting."

I said, "What kind of birds?"

He said, "Quail."

I said, "Man, the best quail huntin' in the whole world is in southwest Mississippi."

We set up the date, and I met this big record executive in Jackson, Mississippi. He landed in the big jet and got off. He had his hunting clothes on, looked like Little Lord Fauntleroy. We got in the car and got on Interstate 55, went on down to the beautiful Versie Ledbetter farm. I drove up in his yard, and said, "Excuse me just a minute, sir. Let me tell Uncle Versie we gonna be huntin' on his place."

I went in, and Uncle Versie was so glad to see me. "Oh, Jerry, God bless you, son. Look, there's seven or eight coveys of birds between here and the road. Boy, I hope you kill a bunch of them. Welcome, son."

I said, "Thank you, Uncle Versie."

I started out of the door and Uncle Versie said, "I'm gonna have to ask you to do something for me, son. Old Della, my mule—I made thirty good crops with her. The veterinarian was out here yesterday to see her and said she's dying. And she's suffering. I just couldn't stand to see him put her to sleep yesterday. Jerry, would you shoot her for me?"

I said, "Yeah, Uncle Versie. I don't like to do it, but if she's suffering I'll shoot her for you."

He said, "Just go ahead and shoot her and go on bird hunting. Me and the boys will tend to her late this evening."

On the way back to the car I said, "I'm gonna have me some fun out of this Hollywood dude."

I got in the car and I said, "You know, that old scoundrel told me I couldn't hunt on his place. Good as I've been to him, he told me, 'No. Get you and that Hollywood slicker away from here.'"

I beat the dashboard with my fist, and I scratched off and throwed rocks all up side of his house. I got on down the road about a hundred yards, and there was old Della in the pasture. I slammed on brakes, and I said, "Unhuh, I'll show that old rascal!" I grabbed my shotgun and I jumped out. Boom! Boom! And down old Della went, graveyard dead.

Just as I turned around and looked over to see what the dude thought, I heard three shots over there. Boom! Boom! Boom!

I said, "Fellow, what are you doing?"

He said, "That old fellow upset you so bad, Jerry, I killed three of his cows."

LITTLE DOGS
AND BIG DOGS

I was raised by a pack of hounds. Why, I wouldn't be here today if it wasn't for them pack of dogs, because they put meat on the table.

Little Dogs and Big Dogs

I was raised by a pack of hounds. Time does not permit for me to name off each one of them and tell a little about each one of them, but I want you to know that everybody referred to that pack of dogs over there at them Clowers' house. Why, I wouldn't be here today if it wasn't for them pack of dogs, because they put meat on the table.

Old Brummy—huge, great big, black and tan hound—had a deep voice. When he barked, he just jarred the ground.

Little Red—fine little old dog. Little Red never would fight, but she'd always get the fight started. Ain't you seen them little dogs, that all they done was wake up them big dogs? I've seen a "huge-mongus," bad, vicious dog laying on the front porch asleep, and me come walking up the walk, and that big old bad dog don't even know I'm there. But a dog big as your fist will jump up and go yelling and hollering and run out there to you scared to do anything. But that little old bitty squealing dog wakes up that old bad dog and he comes and bites your leg.

Old Jennie was a good possum dog. I mean she didn't have no teeth, and in later years I've seen her gum a possum to death. Yes, gum him to death! And Old Tory and Old Big Red.

The awfullest catastrophic dog fight I ever encountered I saw one day with that pack of hounds. I fed them some boiled okra—good old slick, slimy, boiled okra. If you boil that okra, it'll slick up and rope up good now. I eat so much boiled okra when I was a boy I never could keep my socks up.

One day me and my brother, Sonny, come in. We'd been plowing that morning and we come in for dinner. Mama had done cooked up a big pot of that boiled okra. We sat down and eat a bait of it. When we got ready to go back to the field, Mama said, "Boys, them dogs ain't been fed. We don't have nothing here for them but what's left in that bowl of okra. Jerry, take the rest of that bowl of okra and go out there and dump it in the dog pan."

I picked it up and I walked real careful—I didn't want it to slime over on my hands. I went out there in the back yard and I dumped it in the dog pan. Ole Brummy—great big, thunder-barking Brummy—run up there. That okra was so slick, Ole Brummy just—slurp!—sucked it down. It went down so fast he thought the other dog got it, and he jumped on him.

That's the truth! Them dogs fought the rest of the evening, and didn't but one dog know what they was fighting about.

Mike

Mike, an old white American pit bull dog, helped raise me. When I was growing up as a youngun out in the country, Mama would get ready to whip one of us younguns, and she would have to shut Old Mike up in the smokehouse. If she'd draw back to swat one of us, Old Mike would bite her.

You talking about love, one Friday evening I caught the school bus and went home with a friend. When my brother, Sonny, got off the school bus, Old Mike was laying in the front yard and didn't see me get off. He took off after that bus and run it to the end of the line. He watched every youngun get off of it, then laid down under that bus and wouldn't move because I didn't come home on the bus.

My mama and my brother, Sonny, had to hook up the mule and wagon and go over there and just manhandle him up in their arms and load him up on that wagon to bring him home, with him growling and looking back from the back of that wagon toward the school bus.

Now Mike loved me. If that had been some kinfolks, they'd a-said, "Well, he just stopped somewhere."

Little Red

When I was a little boy, one of the prize possessions that I had was a coon dog named Little Red. Little Red, he was the runt of the litter, and I fed him with a bottle. I looked after him, and I worked with him, and he grew up to be an outstanding coon dog. He was a prized possession of mine.

One night we were hunting down in the swamp, and Little Red got cut on a crosscut saw. I picked him up and started crying, and held his back leg where that saw had cut it. Every time his heart would beat, blood would gush from that leg.

We loaded him up in an old rattle-trap Ford car. My brother, Sonny, finally got it cranked. We rushed to McComb, Mississippi, and I was crying and holding my coon dog. We rushed to Gillis's Drugstore, walked up on the sidewalk, and the store was already closed. There was a light on in the back and Mr. Gillis was counting the day's receipts. We bumped on the door, and Mr. Gillis came and opened the door, and said, "What do you boys want?"

There we stood with our overalls on, dog blood all over us, scared to death. My brother, Sonny, said, "Mr. Gillis, we understand there's a veterinarian rents an office from you. Is there any way we can see him? Jerry's coon dog, Little Red, is bleeding to death."

He said, "Boys, I'm sorry, but Dr. Williams is out of town and he won't be back until tomorrow. But bring your coon dog on in my store, put him down on the floor, and let me get the lights on. Let me see if I can help you."

Now some people would have said, "Get that filthy dog off this sidewalk. Look at the blood you done put down here." Yes, they could have run me off and I'd a-hated them the rest of my life. Ever since that night, I been looking for a boy with a hurt dog, because Mr. Norman Gillis showed me how adult people are supposed to set the proper example for young people to follow.

He called his family physician and asked him how to put a pressure bandage on Little Red's leg. He gave him some pills. He said, "Son, you go on home. I'll put your dog on my back porch, and Dr. Williams will see him first thing in the morning."

Little Red lived to hunt again, and I thank God for men like Norman Gillis because he showed a young boy, a little teenager, how adult people are supposed to treat youngsters with problems.

Faster than Highball

Highball was the greatest coon dog that ever lived. I went to the drugstore in Liberty the other day to drink coffee, and somebody said, "Jerry, we've found a coon dog that's better than Highball."

I said, "That's hard to believe."

He said, "Well, I hunted with one about a year ago that's faster than Highball."

That was hard to believe, but this was an honest man. He said, "Yeah, Jerry, he's the fastest dog I ever seen. We took him out to show some people how fast he was and, man, he hit a trail—'Oof! oof! oof!' Then he hit that treed bark—'Ahf, ahf, ahf!!'

"Everybody got there. A man climbed the tree. Everybody went to shining their lights. The man in the tree said, 'I hate to tell you, but there ain't no coon in this tree.'

"The man that owned the dog said, 'See there, this dog's so fast he's done beat the coon to the tree.'"

Bear Bryant of the Litter

I've had a lot to say about Highball. I want you to know Highball was the greatest coon dog that ever lived. Now I ain't ever seen every coon dog. But of any coon dogs that I have ever been associated with, I mean Highball was the Bear Bryant of the litter.

Highball—gritty, big—could strike a cold trail and stay on it, work it. We fed Highball out of an old dinner bell, and that cleared up her voice. That'll do it every time.

One evening a rich doctor from Jackson, Mississippi, had heard of Highball, and he come down and wanted to see this great dog run. We went out in the edge of the swamps, and we turned Old Highball out with some other dogs. Right away Old Highball hit a trail. He worked it slowly until you actually knew Old Highball was seeing the coon, because of all the barking you ain't never heard in your life. You could just know Old Highball was just breathing on the raccoon.

Uncle Versie would holler, "Talk to him. Speak to him!"

But all of a sudden Highball shut up. There was a deathly silence. The doctor said, "What's the matter? What's the matter?"

Uncle Versie Ledbetter said, "Hush, hush. I think I know what's happening. Shut up, listen!"

There was deathly silence for over two minutes. Then, all of a sudden Highball commenced to barking again, just as before.

Uncle Versie said, "Just as I figured, Old Highball was running across posted land."

Old Highball

Uncle Versie Ledbetter's great feat, the one that he was the proudest of, was having a coon dog named Highball. *If I'm lying, I'm dying.* Highball's fame was all over the world. Rich folks would bring coon

dogs there to try to outdo Highball. Highball was known through-
out that country as being the grittiest coon dog in all the world. He
was bad! Man, he'd go in on one anywhere, any time. Highball was
something or 'nother ferocious for awhile! He was bad!

Uncle Versie was down in the swamps hunting one night, and the
biggest coon ever been in Amite River swamps and Highball tied up
in a death-to-death battle. I mean they wallowed down a bunch of
ground there. Uncle Versie hollered, "*Hooo!* Get him, Highball, you
can do it. Highball, you can do it! Put it to him." You could hear
Uncle Versie all over them swamps. "Old Highball, put it on him,
put it on him!"

It ended up in such a ferocious battle that they got up on the
railroad track, and one of them fast trains, the City of New Orleans,
on the mainline of mid-America, run over Highball and that coon
and killed both of 'em graveyard dead while they was fighting.

Uncle Versie commenced to squalling, "*Haw-ooo!*" You could
hear him moaning all over them swamps.

I throwed my arms around him and I said, "Uncle Versie, you got
several other puppies what's the sons of Highball. They'll be as great
as him. Don't cry."

He said, "Boy, I ain't crying 'cause a dog got killed. I ain't that
crazy. The thing that's bothering me is pore Old Highball might a-
died thinking that coon killed him."

Old Blue

I want to tell you about a shore-enough dog named Blue. Uncle
Versie and Aunt Pet Ledbetter bred up Old Blue and trained him to
be their private dog in their later years. All the younguns were gone.
Uncle Versie and Aunt Pet used to go coon hunting, and they bred
Old Blue—a big, stocky bluetick hound—to be vicious where he
could handle a coon by himself. They just took him hunting alone
by himself.

They taught him to be mean. They fed him gunpowder. Uncle Versie fed Old Blue off of a fork, and when he'd reach for that cold biscuit, Uncle Versie would job him with that fork. It made Old Blue mean. They'd go hunting with what we called a possum hunting torch. Get three or four splinters, long, fat pine splinters—now some folks call 'em fat litered splinters. You would hold them splinters together and light one end of the splinters, and it was the cheapest form of lighting in the woods you could find. It took no kerosene, and you didn't have to have no carbide light. So, Uncle Versie and Aunt Pet would get their possum huntin' torch, they'd get Old Blue, and they'd go coon huntin'. Just them three.

Now Old Blue was vicious, as I done told you. One time a limb fell out of a tree; he chewed up the limb. Uncle Versie Ledbetter and Aunt Pet and Old Blue was coon hunting one night—a dry, dry night. It hadn't rained in two months. They was down in the swamps a-hunting. They had that possum hunting torch lit, and Old Blue treed. When Blue trees, it's time to shoot, shake, cut, or climb. Uncle Versie climbed the tree. Old Blue circled around underneath it, just waiting for something to fall. This tree was loaded down with old dried moss; just covered with moss. Uncle Versie got up in the tree and he yelled down to Aunt Pet, "Baby," (it's not uncommon for southern gentlemen to call their womenfolks "Baby") "hold that light up there where I can see its eyes. Higher, hold it higher."

She tiptoed and held it way up. Old Blue's growling. Uncle Versie is up in the top of the tree, looking for the raccoon. "Hey, Baby, there's a stump down there, get up on that stump and hold the light up high. Maybe I can see better then."

She hunkered up on that stump, got up on her toes, and lifted that torch way up. And the fire from that torch caught that dry moss on fire, and it just commenced to consuming that tree!

Uncle Versie started squalling. "Wahhh! Hold Old Blue! Hold Old Blueee!"

Broccoli

I'm so glad the president of the United States has got enough chit-tlins to stand up before the world and say he ain't gonna eat no broccoli. Not only are they telling us we oughta eat broccoli, but they're telling us if we cook our string beans and blackeyed peas with fatback meat in there, it's gonna kill us. Now I can handle a little bit of that broccoli if you smother it in cheese, but I'm here to tell you, if I had a coon dog that wouldn't tree, I'd make him eat broccoli.

Nicki

A dog I have known is named Nicki. I did a CBS special, the "Orange Blossom Special," with Loretta Lynn, Charlie Pride, and Tom T. Hall. (Now Tom T. Hall, by the way, is a great dog lover, head of the humane society in Tennessee, and got dogs what live in castles. He sets that thermostat—all of his dogs are treated just like a hothouse plant.) Me and Tom T., Charlie Pride, and Loretta Lynn did the "Orange Blossom Special" on CBS, ninety minutes. I remember the rating was 32. I recall Frank Sinatra had a special that same week and his rating was 16. I didn't understand the ratings, but at East Fork Consolidated High School I was always taught that 32 was twice better than 16. So I remembered the rating!

Now, I was on this show, off and on, for ninety minutes, and I got nine letters. Fifteen days later, my manager, Tandy Rice, called me and said, "Come to Nashville, you're gonna do a Purina Dog Chow commercial with a dog named Nicki."

I done it in thirty seconds. That's right—thirty seconds. The commercial run one week, and I got *109 letters* wanting to know what kind of dog that was. I got to doing a little researching. I done found out back then that dog was more famous than me. It was a bull terrier, the same dog that was in the movie *Patton*. Nicki was a heap more famous than me. That dog worked by the day, just like I did. Come quitting time he went back to Hollywood, and I went back to Nashville.

Puppy Love

I'm not so sure that none of us have ever been loved by an earthly creature until we have been loved by a dog.

I remember we got a letter from a lady up in Okolona, Mississippi, that said, "Dear Mr. Clower: Please don't rob me of the joy I will receive by giving your little daughter, Katy, a world-famous, black, toy, registered, poodle dog."

Now I wanted this lady to go to work for me. Do you hear how she put it?

She said, "Are you going to rob me of the joy I'm going to have by not letting me give your daughter this dog?"

Now, I knew not to discuss it with Homerline. Sometimes you just need to make a decision on your own and let 'em find out about it after you done done it. I wrote this woman back and said, "Yes, we want the dog." And then I eased into it with Homerline, gradually.

The day was set. We were to go to Okolona to pick up the dog. We drove up the Natchez Trace, got to the lady's house. I found out that this wasn't just no normal dog—I mean this dog's mother was the world-famous show dog, Boogewah PittoDo Lafeet. *Oh, mercy!*

I said, "Is that right?"

"Yeah, and her daddy's more famous than that. He's Mopasaunt Tibbido Lafayette Napoleon."

I said, "Good gracious."

So we got the dog. Driving back down the Natchez Trace, it done come up one of them hurricanes. I mean, the wind and the rain was bad, shoe-mouth deep, windshield wipers a flopping, and you can't see nothing. We're driving home, and Katy is on the back seat holding this beautiful little poodle dog.

Katy said, "What we gonna name it? We've got to have a registered name."

My wife said, "Name it after me—name it "Crazy Trouble": Trouble for what the dog's causing, and Crazy for me having little enough sense to come up here in this hurricane after it."

Katy said, "Mama, the registered name of this little dog will be Katy Burns Clower Tandy Rice Marcel Freckles."

Seeing Eye Dog

There was an old boy went in a Mississippi bank the other day and had a seeing eye dog in front of him. He was holding that dog's harness, and the seeing eye dog just brought that old boy right on in that bank, went around in there and down through a little gate and sat him down in front of a desk in front of a loan officer.

Well, they talked about five minutes and that seeing eye dog come over that desk and eat that banker up. Argh! Arghhh!! I mean bit him good! The blind man grabbed ahold of the harness and out of there they went. Just as they got out on the sidewalk leaving the bank, the dog bit a perfect stranger.

Well, here come the police and they rounding up folks, trying to get witnesses. They got this old blind boy there and was talking to him and said, "Now, look, sir, we understand why the dog jumped over the desk and bit the banker; it was very obvious that he didn't answer your questions properly about your loan. But why would the dog go out of the bank and just bite a perfect stranger?"

He said, "That dog was just getting that bad taste out of his mouth!"

Bilingual Dog

This dog was trotting down the sidewalk hunting a job. He saw a sign in a window: Wanted. A typist, computer operator, and must be bilingual. Well, the dog said, "Woof, woof!" ran into the office, jumped up in the window, got that sign and spit it out on the personnel director's desk. "Woof, woof!"

The man said, "Well, you done brought me this sign. Apparently you think you want this job. You can't type."

The dog run over and got up to the typewriter, and began to run over the letters and was just spitting it out—just done good—and done sixty words a minute. He pulled it out of the typewriter, and handed it to the man.

He looked at it and said, "Hey, sixty words a minute. You didn't even make a mistake; this is fabulous. What about computers?"

The dog went over there and went to popping that little old console and playing that thing, and reams of paper started spinning through there. And it told all about the qualifications of the dog.

The man said, "Well, you sure can type, and you sure can operate a computer, but there's no way you can be bilingual. You must speak at least two languages to have this job."

The dog stood up on his hind legs and looked the man in the eye, and said, "Mee-ow!"

The Lap of Luxury

I drove up to my house the other day, and I saw two beagle hounds laying on my carport. I got out and saw they looked give out. It was very obvious some deer hunter had lost two dogs. Well, I looked on their collars and they said "Dee Barron," and there was a phone number. Well, I went in the house and called the phone number and nobody answered. Then I got to thinking, Dee Barron. I said this Dee Barron has got to be old Uncle Dee Barron's son, grandson, or great-grandson. Since the phone number doesn't answer, I'll just load these old dogs up and go to the old house where Uncle Dee used to live.

I put 'em in the back of my car, they got up on the back seat, and, man, they looked out the window like they thought they was going hunting with me. I took off up the road; it was about five miles up there, and I turned off down the road where Uncle Dee used to live when I was a boy and there was a brick house. The old house was gone. A man was in the back yard raking, and I got out and he said, "Man, you're Jerry Clower."

I said, "That's right. You look like Dee Barron that I growed up with."

He said, "That was my daddy."

I said, "Well, let me ask you something. Do you have a young man that lives here named Dee Barron?"

He said, "Yeah, that's my son."

I said, "Has he got two dogs missing?"

He said, "Yeah, and he is despondent over it. I couldn't hardly get him to go to school this morning 'cause them dogs are missing."

I walked over and opened the back door of my car and them beagle hounds jumped out and barked, and he said, "Oh, you done brought 'em home. He'll be so happy."

He went and put them in the pen, and he turned to me. He said, "Mr. Clower, I want to thank you. And them dogs better be happy and give thanks too, because this is the last time they'll ever ride in a Cadillac."

Crack, W. L., and Rover

There was a man in south Mississippi who was illiterate; he couldn't read or write. He had a boy named W. L. Ledbetter. This old man was Uncle Crack, Uncle Crack Ledbetter. He was a distant cousin to Uncle Versie. Old Man Crack got him a job at the railroad at an early age and saved his money. His life's ambition was to educate his only son, W. L., and send him off to college.

W. L. was a smart young man. He finished high school, and he took the money and caught the City of New Orleans to Batesville,

Mississippi. He got on the bus at Batesville and went to the University of Mississippi at Oxford and enrolled. He was making good grades, but he spent more money than he should have spent. He got to thinking, "What is it I can do to impress my father that he would send me some more money, and wouldn't be griping about me spending so much money up here?"

W. L. got to thinking. "Papa's done sent me a bunch of money, and I done run through it. I like getting in these social things and spending a little money, and eating them foot-long hot dogs."

So, he wrote home and told his mama, that could read, to tell Papa that if he will send old Rover—that dog that he worships, that dog that he thinks more of than me—up here on the train to me with a hundred dollars, I got a professor up here that can teach Old Rover to read.

And that old man went wild. "Whaa, have mercy! Get old Rover ready. Old Rover can learn to read. I ain't never been able to read. I'll have a son and a dog that can read."

He sent old Rover up there with a hundred dollars. Wasn't long, about three months, that hundred dollars run out. The old boy said, "I need me some more money." He wrote his mama again and said, "Send two hundred dollars more. Tell Papa there's a professor up here that can teach old Rover to talk. He actually can say a few words. Send the two hundred dollars."

The old boy graduated. It was time to go home; he done got his degree. He don't know what he's going to do. He's got to figure out something, 'cause the old man done told everybody in town, "The boy's coming home tomorrow and gonna bring Old Rover. Y'all come. He's gonna read and talk to you."

The train pulled into the station and that old man was there with his best suit of clothes on. People got off, the band was playing, everybody was squalling. The old man didn't see W. L. Everybody got off the train, and he looked, and W. L. had got off the last car up there about two hundred yards. The old man run up there and said, "Son, where is Rover? Where is Rover?"

He said, "Papa, I got off up here by myself. I just wanted to share this with you. We was coming along up yonder around the curve. That City of New Orleans was doing ninety-seven miles an hour. Me and Old Rover was sitting there. He was sitting over there on a chair reading the paper, and he was telling me what news was in the paper. Then he lowered that paper down and he looked over at me, and he said, 'W. L. I can't wait to get to your mama to tell her what I saw the maid and your daddy doing one time.'"

W. L. started crying. "Papa, it just infuriated me and made me so mad that a animal that me and you loved much as we loved that dog, would tell a lowdown stinking thing on you like that. Before I knew it, I grabbed him in the collar and I flung him off the back of that train. He hit on them crossties and bounced and went down in a deep ditch. I know it killed him."

The old man looked up and said, "Son, are you sure that lying dog is dead?"

The Coon Huntin' Monkey

When I was growing up, word got out that the best coon hunter in the world was a fellow that lived at East McComb, Mississippi. We done sent him word by the mail rider, "There ain't no coon dog in the world good as Highball. Don't you ever say or tell anybody that there is. We don't believe it none."

Well, we got us up a little contest. They said, "Yeah, this fellow'll catch more coons on a night's hunt than y'all will."

He come driving up in his pickup truck to East Fork School— that's where we met. The fellow let the end gate down on one of them pickups, and there in a cage sitting up in the back of that pickup was a big brown monkey.

Marcel said, "Oh, don't let that thing out. He looks too much like folks to be getting out of there. You leave him up in that pickup truck."

The fellow said, "Y'all don't understand. I use a dog with the monkey. I just want one good tree dog, and I'll show you how to catch more raccoons. Hides are expensive, and I make a good living with that monkey coon huntin'."

Marcel said, "I ain't taking my dog with that trashy thing."

Clovis said, "I'll take old June and we'll go."

So, all of us followed, and old June hadn't gone very far and she treed. Now, any coon hunter will know that sometimes a raccoon will get up in a tree and he'll go out on a limb and jump into another tree, go out on a limb and jump into another tree, and come down way out yonder. That's the art of being a good coon dog; you circle around and make sure he ain't capped the tree. He's up there if you say he's up there!

Well, old June treed. They turned that monkey loose, and people, he had a flashlight in his left hand and a pistol in his right hand, and up that tree he went. *Boogada, booga*, right up that tree. Went all over the tree shining that light with the gun in his hand, looking everywhere, out on each limb, shining, shining. What he would do, he would find the coon and shoot him and the coon would fall out. Well, he didn't find no coon. Down the tree he come, thumbcocked that pistol, put it up to old June's head, Clovis's dog, and said Boom!, just killed him graveyard dead right there.

Clovis said, "Man, what in the world do you mean? That trashy thing has killed my dog."

And the fellow what owned the monkey said, "Clovis, there ain't but one thing that monkey hates worse than a raccoon, and that's a lying coon dog."

PROUD TO BE
AN AMERICAN

 ·

m declaring a war

on negativism. Negativism—I'm sick of it!

The Resort Hotel

You know I ain't gonna lie to you. Since I backed into show business I have been making above-average means, and I never did know how some of the more affluent folks lived. Well, not too long ago I was invited to do a show for some rich folks in a world-famous resort hotel.

Hooo! I got there a day early. Them "yatchies" was tied up in the harbor. Ahhhh! The bellman done met me in a tall hat, had on a clawhammer-tailed coat, got my bags, and helped me up to my room. I walked in the room; there was some German imported chocolates on a silver tray for Mr. Clower's benefit. He hung up my clothes and put my suitcase up, and, man, I'm getting ready to get comfortable. Nebraska and Alabama are going to be playing football on television that afternoon. I had got there a half a day early where I wouldn't miss it. As I went to tip the bellman and hand him the money, I said, "Sir, where is the television at in this room?"

"Oh, sir, we don't have television at this world-famous resort hotel."

I said, "What? Man, they got television at them $8.88 a night places."

"But, sir, you don't understand. Our guests come here not to be disturbed by television."

I said, "Well, I hope they got sense enough to turn it off if they don't want to watch it. I'm gonna see Nebraska and Alabama play, and you rich folks, I done fell out with y'all already."

He said, "Well, the TV room is down close to the lobby.

Now, folks, I had to dress. And what I was wanting to do was put on my loose-fitting pajamas and fix it where my belly could flop around. Rare back, and fix it where that air conditioning unit could blow up this pajama leg and go down that one. And watch Bear Bryant's boys whip up on Nebraska. But I had to dress and go down in the lobby to watch the dadblamed football game.

While I'm down there watching it—it is in the third quarter and it's tied up—in walked four high society women: got them little fancy frizzled britches on, had on a cute little cap, and each one of them had a tennis racket. They come walking in and said, "Oh, sir, we're going to switch the television."

I said, "Ma'am?"

"Oh, yes, the Slim Jim Tournament is on the other station." (Now some kind of "slim" was in there; I remember that distinctly. I think it was somebody named Virginia what was in the Slim tournament, well as I remember.)

I said, "Ladies, I love everybody, but y'all are fixing to read in the morning paper in big headlines all the way across the page, 'GRAND OLE OPRY STAR AND BORN-AGAIN SOUTHERN BAPTIST WHIPS FOUR WOMEN AT THE RICH HOTEL.'"

The Meek Shall Inherit the Earth

Wherever I go, people ask me, "Jerry, was you lying about your football playing days at Mississippi State University?" And I'm a little bit hurt wherever I go if somebody don't rush up to me and say, "Jerry, I remember when you played football at Mississippi State."

Well, I can tell you about a lot of things that happened when I was playing football. One of the reasons I wanted to transfer from Southwest Mississippi Junior College to Mississippi State to play football in the Southeastern Conference was because Mississippi

State played Baylor University—that good Baptist school in the Southwest Conference.

When I was signed to a scholarship at Mississippi State, I called my mama long distance at the country store and had 'em to go over there and get her and bring her over there to the telephone. I said, "Mama, just think, your pore little old country boy is gonna play against the largest Baptist university in the world."

I got ready for them people. I didn't miss prayer meeting for a whole year. I got ready for 'em! I knowed they was the same kinda Baptists I was. *Whooo!* Them folks was ugly to me; I'm telling you! Every Monday morning we would get the scouting report from the coach what scouted the team we was gonna play next Saturday. Well, naturally, when we got ready to play Baylor, I got the scouting report and I looked down hurriedly to see who the man was I was going to play in front of what played for Baylor. *If I'm lying, I'm dying!* You know what it said about a guard named Rayfield? "Big, aggressive, tough; likes to play it mean. In fact, when he was ordained as a Baptist preacher, he had two black eyes."

We played Baylor in Memphis, Tennessee, that year. That Adrian Burke was chunkin' that football! Chunkin' it to a fellow named Isbell. The coach sent word, "Jerry, that quarterback's got too much time to throw the football. You get to him; get to him quick."

I rushed back in there with every fiber of my being. I reached for him, and just before getting my hands on him, that preacher Rayfield hit me on the back of my head, shoved my face down in the dirt and grass, and my bottom lip and bottom teeth just scooped up a big mouthful of that dirt like a dragline. I jumped up, spitting, knocking the grass and the dirt out of my mouth, and I said, "Fellow, you the dirtiest thing I ever played against in all my life. And you're supposed to be a Baptist preacher, playing for Baylor."

He stood up erect. They had done throwed the ball for a touchdown. He popped his hand over his heart, and he pointed his long finger right in my face. He said, "The Bible says, the meek shall inherit the earth."

I had just inherited a mouth plumb full of it, I'll tell you that!

Lay Still

It was the Mississippi State-Alabama game, my last year at Mississippi State. I broke my right hand in the game toward the end of the fourth quarter. Alabama broke out a sophomore running back that day named Geodetti. That was the runningest fellow I have ever seen in my life. He would stop and start and slither and belly back. I've never seen nobody run like he could; he was a running machine. One time he was gone for a touchdown, and he turned around and run back through us just to humiliate us.

I was playing left defense tackle. You put your best linemen there. Back in them days most football teams run to the right, and I was playing left defensive tackle. Butch Abbinger took the snap from the center. Butch pivoted and quick pitched the ball to Geodetti. Here he come around my side. I run over a guard named Mesorani, knocked another guard down named Holdnack, got ahold of Geodetti around the waist. Ah, ha! I knew I had him for a loss, because on the Mississippi State side I could hear them cowbells ringing.

Just as I went to sling Geodetti to the ground, he slithered. Went straight up in the air like you squeeze a watermelon seed. I fell to the ground on my belly, Geodetti come down in my back—just done a little dance around on top of me. Oh, I was hurting! He was stomping me. But he jumped off of me and commenced to running, and I'm laying there on the ground on my belly, beating the ground with my fists.

My teammate, Dog Owens, said, "Jerry, get up and chase him."

I said, "Lay still, he'll be back by here in a minute."

Fifteen-Yard Penalty

I was at Starkville, Mississippi, at a high school game. Right about the middle of the third quarter the official stepped off a fifteen-yard penalty, and stopped right in front of the home team bench.

The coach said, "Referee, you stink. You stink!"

The referee reached down and picked up that red flag and walked fifteen more yards away from him, and said, "How do I smell from here?"

The Inventory

A furnish merchant—that's the individual what you go see in the fall to get financing to make a crop. We got them bankers too, but they won't carry you to the fall. You got to pay so much a month.

When I was a boy we had furnish merchants, and you could go get bacon and barrels of flour and lard from them. The finest furnish merchant I ever knew, I used to call on when I sold fertilizer in Mississippi. He even bought P&G soap by the carload. He let you have whatever you wanted, and he let you pay it back when you sold a bale of cotton.

He had a son, and the son went off to Mississippi State University, got him a degree in accounting, and came back to this old store out in the country where this man had accumulated five thousand acres of land, a cotton gin, sawmill, a feed mill, and this big store. One day the old man got up and went down to his store on Saturday morning, and there was a great big sign up there said, "Closed for Inventory."

He throwed a fit. He hadn't been closed in sixty years. He went around to the side door, got it open, and walked in there and said, "Boy, what's going on?"

The son said, "Papa, we're taking inventory. They taught me this in accounting."

The father said, "Let me tell you something about inventory. You get that ladder and go up yonder in that fur corner and crawl up that ladder and look on that top shelf: you'll see what's left of a bolt of cloth. Me and your mama started sixty years ago with that one bolt of cloth. That's your inventory. Everything else is profit. Now get that door open!"

Big City Vocabulary

You know us country folks in these little small towns, we ain't let these big city folks change our vocabulary. Us country folks, if you go into a store and take something and you break the law, we call it stealing or you are a thief. In them big cities they say shoplifting. I think they are thieves.

I was listening to a big TV "narragator" giving the news in a city of about 300,000, and he said, "A gentleman this morning, in the freezing cold, died from hypothermia."

Well, I switched the TV around and got Greenwood, Mississippi. The TV station there covers about a third of that old bigun I just seen. A fellow came on and said, "Well, I better report to you somebody done froze to death this morning."

A New Bull

This farmer was sitting out in his back yard discussing with his manager about how they had to buy a new bull. It was just imperative that they had to bring some more bloodlines on to the farm. There were three bulls already on the place, and they were out in the lot, and they could hear the guy talking.

The first bull said, "Looka here, I been here three years. There ain't but fifty cows here; thirty of them cows belong to me. I don't care what kinda Mr. Big Shot Bull he brings here, I ain't about to be nice to him."

The second bull said, "I ain't been here but a year and a half, but I agree with you. I ain't about to put up with it. We'll make life miserable for him. And I'll guarantee I ain't about to share nothing with him."

The third bull said, "I ain't been here but six months, and I don't have but about five cows that even like me, but I'll tell you right now, I ain't giving up them five. Mr. Bull's gonna be in a bad state of affairs."

Next day here come one of them big long trucks—great big diesels out on each side of it, smoke belting from it—drove up in the yard, let down the end gate, brakes cut off, that air come off 'em.

There was about the biggest, raunchiest looking old Brahma bull ever been walked off that thing—weighed over a ton—snorting. He didn't have to look through the fence to see the cows grazing down in the pasture. He slapfooted just looked over the fence at them. Great big hump on his back and, man, he just went strutting around the lot. Man, he was something!

The first bull said, "You know, I been doing a little thinking. It was real ugly for me to have the attitude I been having, and I just think I'll share with him."

The second bull said, "You know, I've changed my mind too. I really want to do do the right thing about it."

The third bull busted out of the stall, run out in the lot, commenced to pawing the ground, whiskers up on his back, just trotting around out there, pawing in the dirt.

The first bull said, "Hey, man, what in the world you doing? You crazy? That thing'll kill you."

He said, "Look, I just wanta make for sure that he knows that *I'm* a bull!"

Clower Takes a Trip

A while back I got a telephone call. I picked up the phone and said, "This is Jerry Clower from Yazoo City, Mississippi, talkin'."

This man said, "I'd like to know if you would come and speak to the Cattle Feeders Association in California."

I said, "Sir, where are you having your meeting?"

He said, "Yosemite National Park."

I said, "Yo-seh-mite—that's a wonderful place."

He said, "It's Yo-*sem*-i-te."

I said, "Naw sir, Miss Robinson at East Fork Consolidated High School, at Route 4, Liberty, Mississippi, taught me that that was Yo-seh-mite. And as well as I remember, that ain't too far from the Mojave desert."

He said, "Well, sir, I don't know how much it'll cost to get you out here, but we need you to come and speak to us."

So me and Mama flew out there on one of them big Delta jets. Now that was about the finest trip I have ever took in all my life. I been criticizing some of the young men in this country about the hairdo they have, but y'all oughta seen the hairdo of them ladies what was serving folks on that airplane. It beat all I ever heard of in all my lifetime.

One of them ladies had her hair whipped around over her right eye and then down. She was blind in her right eye. Then she had three strands of hair pulled around across this left eye right here, and she was coming down the aisle walking and stepping real high, just like a blind bridle on a brand new mule.

I said, "Lady, if you don't get that hair out of your face so you can see where you're going, you're gonna scald somebody with that hot coffee."

I want to tell you something else, there ain't no sense in them wearing them dresses as short as they were wearing them, I'll tell you that. As long as she stood straight, and walked straight and normal, it was all right, but when she reached up to get a pillow up in that overhead rack—there ain't no sense in that. After she reached and got the first pillow, I was the only man on there what didn't ask for a pillow then.

Neighbor's Rabbit

One morning Homerline was washing dishes, and she looked out the back window and went to screaming.

I said, "Honey, what in the world is the matter?"

She said, "Look at Old Duke!" (That was my bassett hound.)

Duke was standing there holding a rabbit in his mouth; done killed it. And I recognized right off it was Jack and Eugenia's pet rabbit from next door. "What in the world are we gonna do?"

Homerline went and got the rabbit and brought him in the house and bathed him, blow-dried him with the hair dryer, fluffed him up, took him back over there, put the rabbit back in the pen, shut the gate, and come on back in the house.

Well, the following Saturday it was a routine thing that Jack and Eugenia and Homerline and me would drink coffee about ten o'clock. So we was sitting in there drinking coffee and Eugenia said, "Y'all know, the strangest thing happened. Our rabbit died, and we buried the thing. Two days later we go out there in the backyard, and there's that rabbit, back in the pen. Looked like he just come from the beauty parlor."

Apple Pie and Coffee

One of the wonderful things about living in Yazoo City, Mississippi, is that we are on the Yazoo River, not far from the Mississippi River, and we have a lot of people who came from other countries to Yazoo City. One of their kinsman showed up the other day and he couldn't speak a word of English, not one word. This immigrant went to his uncle and he said, "Hey, I just got here, I don't know how to ask for nothing to eat."

He said, "Well, I think I can teach you to say 'apple pie and coffee.' That's simple nourishment, and I believe I can teach you to say that right, and you can go on down to the cafe and get you some. Say 'ap-pull pie, coff-fee.'"

He said, "Ap-pull pie, coff-fee."

So he went down to the restaurant.

"What'll you have?"

"Ap-pull pie, coff-fee."

"Yes, sir."

He ate that for three weeks. He went back to his uncle, said, "Hey, I'm burnt out on that."

"Well, I'll teach you to say 'ham sandwich—hammm sand-wiitch.'"

He said, "Hammm sand-wiitch."

"That's good."

He went down to the cafe, waiter came up, had that towel hung over his arm, said, "What'll you have?"

He said, "Hammm sand-wiitch."

Old boy said, "White or rye?"

"Hammm sand-wiitch."

"White or rye?"

"Hammm sand-wiitch!!"

He said, "Look, bud, make up your mind. You want it white or rye?"

The poor fellow looked up and said, "Ap-pull pie and coff-fee."

Bill's Vacation

We have a negative barber in my town. You go in his barber shop when the sun's shining bright and say, "Pretty day today, ain't it?"

He'll say, "It'll be raining in an hour." If I wasn't a Christian, I'd hire somebody to kill him.

My buddy Bill went in that barber shop. That old pessimistic barber said, "Bill, I hear you gonna take a trip."

Bill said, "Yeah, I'm gonna catch TWA airlines, I'm gonna fly to Rome, and I'm gonna visit with the pope."

That old pessimistic barber said, "TWA's the sorriest airline in the world; they'll lose your suitcase. They ain't never on time. If you make it to Rome on that old sorry airline, Rome stinks this time of the year. And you ain't gonna get to see the pope. If you see the pope, you're gonna stand down there with 100,000 people, all hunkered up together, hoping that that pope walks out on a little old shelf way up yonder on the side of the wall. That's as close as you'll ever get to the pope."

Well, old Bill was back in the barber shop in about a month. That old pessimistic barber said, "Bill, you didn't take that stupid trip, did you?"

Bill said, "I did take that trip, and you lied to me. TWA was a good airline. They didn't lose my suitcase; they was right on time. Them flight attendants was friendly, we landed in Rome, took a whiff of Rome, and Rome wasn't stinking. You were right about one thing; there was 100,000 people all scrooched up hoping that the pope would make his appearance on that shelf way up there on the side of the wall."

That old pessimistic barber said, "Bill, you didn't get to see him either, did you?"

Bill said, "I did do it. While I was standing there hoping that pope would make his appearance up there on that porch, a fellow come walking up to me and grabbed me by the arm and said, 'Hey buddy, come with me. The pope sent me after you.'

"We went around there and got on an elevator and went up three floors and the elevator stopped and the door opened. There stood the pope! I said, 'Brother Pope, this is the highlight of my trip, to get to see you one on one.'"

That old pessimistic barber said, "Bill, why did the pope pick you out of all them folks to bring you up there as an individual?"

Bill said, "I wondered the same thing and I asked the pope why he sent for me. The pope said, 'Young man, I wanted to pray with you and counsel with you, because out of 100,000 people, you undoubtedly got the sorriest haircut of anybody we ever saw.'"

The Hitchhiker

When I was a student at Mississippi State University, a traveling salesman up and left Starkville, Mississippi, and went over into west Alabama and was calling on customers. He got sick and died. Well, they dispatched a hearse from the funeral home in Starkville to go pick up this traveling salesman.

They loaded him up and two fellows started back to Starkville with him. They stopped in Columbus about sundown to get a Coca-Cola. The man that wasn't driving said, "I'm just going to stay in the hearse. I'll watch the body. I don't want nothing."

The driver got out, went to the restroom, got him a Coke, and while he was gone a fellow come up and pecked on the glass. The man sitting in the hearse said, "May I help you?"

He said, "I need a ride to Starkville bad. I see an Oktibbeha County tag on this hearse and, man, I need to get home. It's an emergency."

The fellow said, "Well, man, we've got a body back there in the back, and this is just a two-seater up here. There's no way you can ride with us unless you get back there with the corpse."

He said, "Man, I'll hang on to the top of this thing if you will let me get back to Starkville. I need a ride bad."

He said, "Well, I'll open the back door for you. You scrooch down, sit down right here in this corner, right behind the driver, and we'll give you a ride." The man got settled, and the driver come out of the restroom, sat down and took off, doing about eighty-five miles an hour. The other man ain't told the driver about the hitchhiker.

That thing was just eating that prairie country up to Oktibbeha County, Mississippi. That big old Cadillac just flew across there. Suddenly this hand come through the curtain and grabbed the driver of the hearse, and he said, "Buddy, is it all right to smoke back here?"

The driver just opened the door and stepped out.

Salesman at the Funeral

I love salesmen. This traveling salesman got into this town in the middle of the afternoon. It was a town of about 12,000 to 15,000 people, and there wasn't a soul nowhere. The man got to looking, and every business establishment in the city was closed. He kept looking and couldn't find a living human being. He went to the fire station and there stood one little teenage boy.

The boy said, "They made me stay here with a two-way radio where I can call 'em if I see smoke."

The salesman said, "Where is everybody?"

The boy said, "They're at the graveyard having a funeral. One of the most prominent men ever lived in this city; they burying him this afternoon."

Well, this fellow wanted to go out there, 'cause when a whole town shuts down because one of their citizens died, he must be a hoss. The old boy went out there, and he stood back of the crowd. The preacher got up and preached the funeral. They was all at the graveyard 'cause the church house couldn't hold them.

The preacher said, "I wonder if there is anybody here would like to say anything about our departed brother."

Nobody said a word.

Then the traveling salesman stepped forth, and he said, "Sir, Mr.

Jones must have been a wonderful, respected man, and I'm just in awe of so many turning out for the funeral. But if none of y'all have anything you want to say, I'd like to take this opportunity to say a few words about Red Man chewing tobacco."

Hog Feed

There was a feed salesman the other day called on one of them old hard-headed pork producers. The man had three hogs in a pen— piney woods rooters. I'm talking about great big, high-arched-back, pork-rib-shining animals.

The feed salesman said, "Sir, I got the finest feed on the market: homogenized, pelletized, water soluble. Every mouthful of that hog ration is exactly what that hog needs. You need to buy some of this. I learned when I was studying in college that you can grow three 200-pound hogs for the same feed that you can grow one 400-pound hog. Sir, you need to buy some of my hog feed. Look at them three little old hogs. How old are they?"

The man said, "Eight months old."

The feed salesman said, "Why, you could take my feed and get them hogs finished out in just four months. Wouldn't that please you? Wouldn't you rather have the hogs finished in four months in place of eight months?"

And the man said, "What in the world is time to a hog?"

The Maddest Man I Ever Saw

The maddest fellow I ever heard of was riding the train, the Panama Limited—main line of mid-America, the Illinois Central Railroad, what runs from New Orleans to Chicago and back. There was a man stepped on the bottom step of that train in McComb, Mississippi, and turned around to kiss his mama goodby, and kissed a bull in the mouth at Hammond, Louisiana. When that thing takes off, it takes off!

A traveling salesman got on that train in Chicago, headed south. He told the porter, "I'm afraid to go to sleep because I may not wake up in time to get off this train in Winona, Mississippi, in the morning."

The porter said, "You ain't got nothing to worry about. That's why I'm on the train—to wake you up. I'll be glad to wake you up. Not only will I wake you up, but I'll hand you a good hot cup of coffee. You'll be bright-eyed, ready to make your calls in Winona, Mississippi, in the morning."

The traveling salesman said, "Sir, you don't understand. I'm hard to wake up, and if you call me and I don't answer you, and you shake me, I have been known to come up fighting."

The porter said, "That's all right. I've had this job forty years. I fight somebody every morning. I don't care how much resistance you give me, I don't care how much you fight, if you tell me to put you off the train, I'll put you off."

Well, the man slept good. When he woke up the next morning the train was sitting still in the station. He raised the drape to see where he was and he saw a sign, McComb, Mississippi. That's two hours south of Winona! He throwed a fit. Them veins stood out on the side of his neck, and turned blood red. He grabbed the porter in the throat and choked him. He was so mad he slapped a crippled fellow down on the train. Police came aboard, just manned him down. They got out there between them railroad cars, fighting with him, and him kicking rocks and screaming and hollering. They called the president of the Illinois Central Railroad and said, "We got a maniac on our hands. How do you want us to handle him?"

The president of the railroad said, "It's your fault. You're the one who didn't wake him up. You give him whatever money he lost 'cause you didn't wake him up, and you put him on the next northbound train NOW!"

Well, they calmed the fellow down, and the train pulled out to New Orleans.

That police reached in his pocket, took out his handkerchief, and started daubing the blood and the sweat where that mad fellow had clawed him. He said, "You know that's the maddest human being I ever seen in my life. Don't you agree?"

The porter said, "He was a mad fellow, but I've seen one other man in my life madder than him."

He said, "Who in the world could that have been?"

The porter said, "The man I put off in Winona this morning!"

Feudin' Stars

I been to Hollywood, and I did the "Family Feud" show. (No, Richard Dawson did not kiss me, thank the Lord.) The Grand Ole Opry stars played for charity. The problem is, they go out and they interview a hundred folks and they ask them questions. Them hundred folks answer the questions, then they let people get on "Family Feud," they ask them the same questions, and if they answer like them hundred folks did, then they win a bunch of money.

The Grand Ole Opry stars played the Western stars. Let me tell you who the Grand Ole Opry stars were: Ricky Scaggs, Larry Gatlin, Jeannie Pruett, Bill Anderson, and Jerry Clower. Standing over there representing the Western stars was Dennis Weaver (old "Mc-Cloud"); Festus from "Gunsmoke"; next to him was Amanda Blake, that woman what run the beer joint on "Gunsmoke"; and next to Miss Kitty was Doug McClure of "The Virginian"; then Dale Robertson of "Wells Fargo"; then old Pat Buttram of "Green Acres." We got it on, and we played.

It ain't all that funny after you get on there. Some of them folks were dumb. They asked Jeannie Pruett to name a fish good to eat. She said, "Bass." Two people out of a hundred had said bass!

They asked us the question, "What do you put under your pillow?" We said, "Gown. Pajamas." Dale Robertson said, "Gun." That may tell us where we're headed—that was one of the answers the hundred folks had given, too. But you know what twelve people out of a hundred said? "Wedding cake." Ever heard of that?

Larry Gatlin said, "I'm leaving. I ain't staying around nobody this dumb."

I got to thinking: who in the world would want to lay up there with their head on a pillow knowing them ants was after that icing up under there?

I used to sit at home with my belly flopping, barefooted, and answer every question. Every question I didn't know, my wife could tell me what it was, and wham! we had it.

Let me play it with you for just a moment. Richard Dawson said, "Name a fruit that starts with a *P*."

Ricky Scaggs said, "Pear." That was one of the answers.

Larry Gatlin said, "Persimmon." That was wrong.

Jeannie Pruett said, "Pineapple." That was one of the answers.

Come to Bill Anderson, he's from Georgia. He said, "Peach." That was the number one answer.

Come to me, I said, "Plum."

"Jerry, that's one of the answers."

Come back to Ricky Scaggs, he didn't know. Come to Bill Anderson, he said, "Papaya." That was one of the answers.

Come to me, last one, $11,000 for the Grand Ole Opry Trust Fund. "You can do it, Jerry, you can do it. Come on, Jerry, and knock 'em in the creek. Last one, fruit that starts with a *P*. Three seconds, two seconds. . . ."

I said, "Pernana."

How to Tell Time

There was a fellow stopped by a dairy farm down in south Mississippi the other day. He was lost. He walked out to the milk barn, and this old boy had his head in that cow's flanks, and he was getting with it, milking that cow. This old boy said, "Howdy!"

The fellow looked around and he asked, "Which way is it to Bogue Chitto?"

The old boy said, "Go back to the highway, and go due east. When you get to Interstate 55 turn north, go about six miles, and you'll see the exit to Bogue Chitto."

The fellow said, "Well, thank you, sir. Can you tell me what time it is?"

That old boy reached his hand up under the udder of that cow, let them sookums hang down between his fingers, and he eased that udder up, and he kept pushing it up. He kept pressing his head down against that cow flank, and he said, "Twenty minutes till four." He dropped the udder and started again—zinga, zinga, zinga.

The fellow said, "Wait a minute. Can you reach up under there and feel that cow's udder and tell the time?"

"Certainly. Want me to teach you how to do it?"

"I shore do. Get up. Let me set down on that stool."

"All right, put your hands up under there and scatter them out. Let them sookums drip down." That fellow sat down and he eased his hands up under there and he got 'em in position.

The old boy said, "All right now, raise up on that udder—little more pressure. Put your head down. Lift up, lift up. Now! Can't you see that clock on the wall right over there?"

Procto

In 1969 I was selling fertilizer down in Florida. I pulled a muscle in my side. I run to the nearest airport and caught me a jet airplane to Jackson, Mississippi. I got in my car, and I rushed to Kings Daughters Hospital in Yazoo City, Mississippi. They paged Dr. Chapman: "Dr. Chapman, come to the emergency room." They stuck a thermometer in my mouth. I said: "I pulled a muscle in my side."

He said, "That spot down there, Jerry, is hot. You have a high temperature. I'm going to have to give you a series of tests. I think you have diverticulitis. After this series of tests I can tell you for shore whether you got diverticulitis or not."

Now, folks, I done told y'all that I love you. Listen to me well. If you go to the hospital for any reason and you remotely think you hear somebody say, "procto," don't let 'em get near you. You gather your split-tail gown around you and you go hide in the nearest swamp. They ain't strapping me again to a sawhorse, turning me bottom side upwards, unbritching a .410 gauge shotgun (they did take the sight off the barrel).

I changed my will after that happened to me. It is written in my will that my wife, if she ever allows that to be done to me again, will never spend a dime of my money. Never!

The Chauffeur and the Professor

A few years ago at the Independent Oil Dealers Association of America in Houston, Texas, there was a speaker, a technical fellow with a Ph.D. from the School of Mines. Ah, he shelled down the corn; he was brilliant. He made them oil people really believe they were something.

When he got done, there was a standing ovation. They just bellowed and hollered and run up to him and said, "Sir, we need a public relations venture now right bad for the oil industry. Please take a sabbatical from your school. We'll put you in a limousine with a chauffeur, and wherever we can get a crowd of people, we want you to talk to them and say the wonderful things about the oil industry you just said to us."

The man took the job. He had been out on the road about five months. One day they are going down the highway, and the chauffeur looks in the rearview mirror at the professor on the back seat and says, "Sir, there ain't no justice in this country. I can make that speech better than you. I can! I've heard you make it a hundred times, and I've memorized it. I'm a better speaker than you. You are making so much money you can't spend it all, and I go hungry, just driving this car. I guarantee I can make a speech as good as you, and I ought to get a raise."

The professor said, "My dear fellow, I have my Ph.D., and I don't want to hear all that."

The chauffeur said, "I don't care where you got all that stuff. I can make the cotton-picking speech better than you."

The professor said, "Pull in at a roadside park up here. The school where I'm going, they don't know me. I'll swap clothes with you and let you get up there and make the speech and make a fool out of yourself, and I'll break you from sucking eggs right here."

"Suits me fine," the chauffeur said. "Get your britches off."

They changed clothes, went on into the university. There were 22,000 people in the field house. The real professor was sitting on the back row of the auditorium, with his chauffeur's cap in his lap.

Here's the chauffeur with the professor's suit on, up on the stage. Now you talking about making a talk! Whooo-eee!! Them students hollered, they rolled on the floor, they bellowed, they screamed. *He shucked the corn right on down to the cob.* He forever more inflamed them.

The president of the university got up and said, "Now, students, we have a few minutes before the bell rings. I wonder if you would like to ask this learned gentleman any questions."

Well, you know the type—a real egghead—got up about halfway back. He had them horn rim glasses on, had a book under each arm. He said, "Professor, if a dinosaur died two billion years ago, and the earth's stratosphere built up over that carcass, and today on a wild-cat drilling venture a drill bit passes through that decayed carcass at 8,943 feet, what will be the name of that stratosphere? And what will be the pH of that soil contained in the drill bit?"

That old boy on that stage stared right at him. He said, "Long as I've been in this business I ain't never been asked a question that simple. Just to show you how simple that question is, my chauffeur is in the back of the room, and I'm going to ask him to stand up and answer it!"

My New House

I built a new house at Route 4, Liberty, Mississippi, and I put a chimney in it. Every wire is underground. The rural electric people dug a trench and put the wires underground—I don't have a wire running inside my house. I was so proud of everything. The telephone wires, the TV wires, the electric cooperative—they're all underground. You drive up and there's a house sitting in the middle of forty acres and no wires going into it. I like that.

So, I was wanting to make sure the guy who built my chimney knew what he was doing, so that it would draw like my grandpapa used to have. I said to the old boy building the chimney, "Man, will this chimney draw?"

He said, "You got one bad problem. I see you got a small dog. You'll have to keep him chained, because he'll be sucked up this chimney."

The Greatest Disservice

The greatest disservice the United States Congress has ever done to the American citizens was when they allowed some egghead judge to bust up the telephone service. That beats all I ever saw that the American people would have been mistreated as bad as we were mistreated by that telephone stuff. . . .

I dialed to get a phone put in my new house, and got a town three hundred miles from me. I said to the operator, "Darling, I got the wrong number."

"Oh no. We'll get the work order down there."

And I used to have a telephone man in my church. He sang solos in my church. He was a godly fellow, a good neighbor. I saw him the other day, and he's retired. I said, "Please don't make me call eighty-seven different numbers to try to get me a telephone."

He said, "You can't get a telephone from the phone company. They don't have telephones. If you got to buy a phone, I'd suggest Radio Shack."

I said, "Who done this?"

He said, "The judge."

Well, we oughta have an uprising and march in the streets!

A Compliment on Us

In the last few weeks I've had my battery charged. Oh, this is such a great country. I thank God for the privilege of living in the United States of America. Things have happened just recently to bolster my thankfulness that I am an American.

I'm sitting on the couch the other evening watching TV—and it shows a bunch of folks standing in line, and they had been in line for four and five hours, in the freezing ice and snow in Russia, to get a McDonald's hamburger. Super power! And when them folks stood in line freezing, and they finally got their Big Mac, they stuck them old styrofoam dishes up under their clothes and took them home with them.

You know that kind of woke me up. I said, "Jerry, you might not be thankful enough. When I get a Big Mac, it takes me about five seconds, and I'm driving a four-door Brougham." I don't ever remember driving off and holding up that Big Mac, and saying, "Lord, thank you I ain't had to stand in no line in no ice and snow to get this hamburger."

So that's a compliment on us. We done bought billions of Big Macs and never had to stand in the ice and snow.

Negativism

I'm declaring war on negativism. Negativism—I'm sick of it. I was interviewed backstage at the Grand Ole Opry last Saturday night, and there stood an NBC News "narragator." He had a microphone and one of them recorders hanging on his shoulder. He said, "Jerry, I'm interviewing Grand Ole Opry stars, those who may be booked in Europe this summer. I'm sure that you are afraid of them terrorists and you will cancel any bookings you have overseas."

I said, "Sir, you are just as wrong as you can be. Khadafi ain't gonna control my life, I ain't no wimp, and I'll fly to Europe whenever I dadblamed please." I said, "Sir, the major lines are class people. If they feel they can risk their captain and the co-pilot and their flight attendants to fly on an airplane, old Jerry will go with them. I will not cancel."

This fellow was real shook because he was wanting to talk negative about that. He was wanting to say, "Ain't nobody going to Europe, ain't going to spend nothing," and I shook him up.

He said, "Mr. Clower, what if them terrorists blow up the airplane you're on?"

I said, "I got a home in heaven."

He said, "Well, what if them terrorists kidnap you?"

I said, "I'll get Jesse Jackson to come get me!"

Proud

It ain't complicated—the first Bible story I ever remember studying in Sunday school. It dawned on me immediately and I have remembered it the rest of my life: a man was walking along minding his own business and a bunch of robbers jumped on him, stripped him naked, left him half dead, and throwed him in the ditch.

He got excited when he saw a fellow coming. He said, "There

comes some help." But the fellow walked right on by. Then he got excited again, he saw somebody else coming; but they even crossed the road to get away from him.

Then here come another fellow, the Good Samaritan. He went down in the ditch and bathed his face, poured some oil on him, give him a little wine, helped him up, put him on a mule, and took him to the motel. He paid for his lodging, left some money at the front desk for room service, and said, "I'm gonna come back and check on you in a few days."

Kuwait was the person who got mugged and left half dead and throwed in the ditch. Others just ignored him, but the United States of America, that country that I am privileged to live in, was the Good Samaritan. We went to the aid of Kuwait, the person who was robbed and mugged. And we straightened out the man, Saddam Hussein, who mugged him.

I've never been prouder to be an American in my life.